MY YEARS AS A
WAR
CORRESPONDENT

MY YEARS AS A
WAR
CORRESPONDENT

A Vietnam War Story

JEAN CLAUDE MARTIN

Although the author has made every reasonable effort to ensure that the information in this book is correct, the author does not assume and hereby disclaims any liability to any party for any loss, damage, or disruption caused by errors or omissions, whether such errors or omissions result from negligence, accident, or any other cause. Names, characters, businesses, places, and events are either the products of the author's imagination or are used in a fictitious manner. All historical persons and events are written in the interpretation and understanding of the author and do not claim to be absolute truth.

Copyright © 2023 by Jean Claude Martin, Ltd.

All rights reserved. No part of this book may be reproduced or transmitted in any form or by any means, electronic or mechanical, including photocopying, recording, or any information storage and retrieval system, without permission in writing from the author.

ISBN: 979-8-9889031-0-9 - Paperback
eISBN: 979-8-9889031-1-6 - eBook

Printed in the United States of America

∞This paper meets the requirements of ANSI/NISO Z39.48-1992 (Permanence of Paper)

080723

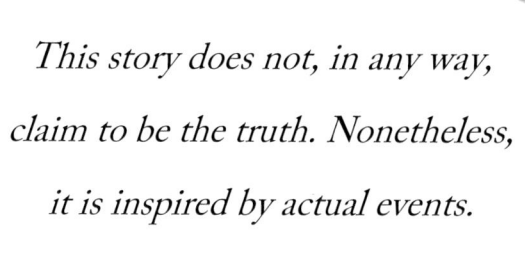

This story does not, in any way, claim to be the truth. Nonetheless, it is inspired by actual events.

Contents

Character List   IX
Preface   XIII

CHAPTER 1	Praise God	1
CHAPTER 2	Going to Pak Nhai	11
CHAPTER 3	Beginning of My Story, Two Years Earlier	19
CHAPTER 4	Getting Ready	25
CHAPTER 5	Fort Bragg Boogie	27
CHAPTER 6	Train Ride to Fort Bragg	31
CHAPTER 7	Going to 'Nam, June 1967	37
CHAPTER 8	Nha Trang Airport Headquarters	43
CHAPTER 9	Meeting with Lieutenant Colonel Steve Miller	47
CHAPTER 10	Training in France	55
CHAPTER 11	Hanoi	61
CHAPTER 12	The Banquet	65
CHAPTER 13	The Interview	71
CHAPTER 14	Ho Chi Minh Trail	75
CHAPTER 15	Road to Pak Nhai	87
CHAPTER 16	Recovery	91
CHAPTER 17	Colonel Gorky's Second Interview	95
CHAPTER 18	Colonel Gorky's Safe House	105
CHAPTER 19	Making New Friends	109
CHAPTER 20	New Lover	113
CHAPTER 21	Going to the Palace	121
CHAPTER 22	The Handover	125
CHAPTER 23	Princess Bopha Sovannar	133

CHAPTER 24	The Palace	**139**
CHAPTER 25	The Pile of Maps	**145**
CHAPTER 26	Going to Pak Nhai, Cambodia	**155**
CHAPTER 27	Into South Vietnam	**159**
CHAPTER 28	Part One	**163**
CHAPTER 29	Part Two	**181**
CHAPTER 30	Nha Trang Map	**185**
CHAPTER 31	Chiphu, Cambodia	**189**
CHAPTER 32	Củ Chi Tunnel Complex	**195**
CHAPTER 33	Finding My Way	**201**
CHAPTER 34	Nha Trang	**205**
CHAPTER 35	Interrogation on a US Navy Ship	**211**
CHAPTER 36	Lima Site 85, Northeast Laos	**223**
CHAPTER 37	Khe Sanh Valley	**225**
CHAPTER 38	Battle of Nha Trang	**227**
CHAPTER 39	Back to Chiphu, Cambodia	**235**
CHAPTER 40	Back to Pak Nhai, Cambodia	**239**
CHAPTER 41	Back to the Palace, Vientiane, Laos	**243**
CHAPTER 42	Heading to France	**251**
CHAPTER 43	Heading for Boston	**257**
CHAPTER 44	Finding Sofie Solberg	**261**
CHAPTER 45	Heading to Norway	**267**

Conclusion *273*
Glossary *275*
Acknowledgments *277*

Character List

USA

- John William Wilson: main character; alias: Jean Claude Martin
- Sofie Solberg: John Wilson's love interest
- Mr. Wilson: John Wilson's father
- Mrs. Wilson: John Wilson's mother
- Paul: John Wilson's brother
- Mary: Paul's wife and John Wilson's sister-in-law
- Mr. Richard Smith: oil man in Woodstock
- Mrs. Mary Smith: wife of an oilman
- Mary Jean Eaton: John Wilson's sister
- Herb Eaton: Mary's husband and John Wilson's brother-in-law
- Debby Loewen: first daughter of Mary and Herb Eaton
- Kim Black: second daughter of Mary and Herb Eaton
- Kris Pruneau: third daughter of Mary and Herb Eaton
- Fred Clark: accountant for the Woodstock ski areas in the winter months and a bartender at the Woodstock Country Club in the summer months
- Robert Clark: president of the Woodstock National Bank and brother of Fred Clark

- Mr. and Mrs. Paul Pyix: French ski manufacturer who visited Woodstock, Vermont, and lived in Thonon-les-Bains, France

SOUTH VIETNAM

- Captain Massey: An Khe 1st Air Cavalry Main Base Headquarters commander.
- William Coleman: CIA Deputy Director for Southeast Asian Theater
- Colonel Black: Nha Trang First Field Force Headquarters intel officer
- Brigadier General Palmer: First Field Force head personnel officer
- Mr. Dinh: Handler in Nha Trang
- Lieutenant Colonel Steve Miller: Nha Trang First Field Force Headquarters intel officer
- Ms. Kim: Main handler in Saigon, restaurant owner in Cho Lon Chinatown.
- Mr. Chi: asset/cleaner in Nha Trang disguised as a cyclo driver
- Mr. Long: gave me food and a motorcycle ride into Saigon during the Tết Offensive
- Sterling Stefferson: friend and professional photographer

FRANCE

- Colonel Winter: French commander of the training camp

- Ms. Monet: asset, camp trainer, and lecturer in France with Colonel Winter

HANOI, NORTH VIETNAM

- Colonel Dima Gorky: Russian officer and KGB agent of the Committee for State Security; architect of the Vietnam War and training camps for the North Vietnamese Army elite special forces, Laos forces, and Cambodia forces
- Colonel Nguyen Cong Ho: Architect of all the supply trails and tunneling in Laos, Cambodia, and borders along western Vietnam
- Mr. Hong: main handler in Hanoi
- Ms. Hue: female escort on Hanoi trip to Dien Bien Phu
- Mr. Dang: male escort on Hanoi trip to Dien Bien Phu
- Mr. Claude Barnet: ambassador of France
- Mrs. Therese Barnet: wife of the ambassador of France
- Major Tuan Vu: commander of the first convoy that left Hanoi and went down the Ho Chi Minh trail with suppliers and military personnel

CAMBODIA

- Bopha Sovannar: princess of Cambodia; special friend of Colonel Gorky
- Lieutenant Anh: officer of the quartermaster in Colonel Gorky's compound in Cambodia

- Ms. Sing: nurse at Colonel Gorky's Compound medical clinic.
- Doctor Loi: doctor at Colonel Gorky's compound medical clinic
- Mr. Cuong: main handler in Pak Nhai, Cambodia
- Lieutenant Colonel Pham: commanding officer of the NVA and Viet Cong in Chiphu, Cambodia, sector
- Captain Duc: NVA officer with Lieutenant Colonel Pham; traveled with Jean Claude to Saigon
- Lieutenant Bein: company headquarters office under Lieutenant Colonel Pham's command

LAOS

- Angelina Vongkhamchanh: Jean Claude's serious girlfriend and daughter of the prince of Laos
- Mr. Tong: handler at French Embassy in Vientiane, Laos
- Lieutenant Minh: with the first convey under Major Vu's command
- Major Tran: took command of the platoon when Major Vu was killed

NORWAY

- Mrs. Bjorn Solberg: Sofie's mother in Bergen, Norway

PREFACE

8-20-2023

To Lisa

TO JOURNEY IS TO LIVE

Jean Claude Martin

Photograph by Sterling Stefferson

I have a story to tell you. It's a long adventure with a lot of twists and turns. Traveling to different countries—France, Switzerland, Norway, Vietnam, Laos, Cambodia, and Thailand—we will melt into their cultures, experiencing in their folk dancing, singing, music, food of the regions, and just having fun.

You will experience relationships—meeting the royal family of Laos and an operative KGB officer and how we developed adventurous tales of mystery, drama, trust-building, and narrow escapes—romance, jealousies, disappointments, deceptions, and achievements.

You will read about espionage, spying, hand-to-hand combat, brutal battlefield death, and how to disguise appearances and move around damaged encounters.

CHAPTER 1
PRAISE GOD

As a French war correspondent, I was assigned by the US Intelligence group to gather all intelligence from the North Vietnamese Army (NVA) and any allies of the North Vietnamese communist regime. I received months of training at United States military forts and a special French espionage school, where I learned how to handle top secret intelligence materials and pass this intel to the authorities and how to write about the war effort to the American forces and their allies. My focus was on the North Vietnamese government and the struggle for the unification of the North and South.

Our campsite was in a small open field at the edge of the jungle. The sun was up and shining brightly, already warming up the crispy morning. I could almost smell the air coming from Pleiku in South Vietnam to the east. The fog was lifting off a small stream as I approached its banks. The jungle was full of music from the birds, and monkeys were squealing in the distance.

I was going to a waterfall about two hundred yards from our campsite to wash up and take a quick shower before breakfast. I didn't know when I'd have a chance to take another shower—it could be days and I didn't want to smell like a water buffalo to others.

I felt my surroundings were safe, and I was at peace with my morning activities. The water had a soft and cold feeling on my body. The soap I had made great bubbles as I rinsed in the waterfall. I looked downstream

and noticed a few residents at the other end of the waterfall pool. I let the alligators know I wasn't intruding on their territory. Finally, I got dressed and prepared to walk back to the camp.

While I walked toward the camp, the jungle came alive with small arms fire and rocket-propelled grenade rounds (RPGs) blasting the camp to smithereens. I could hear people talking while others were screaming at the top of their lungs. I heard bullets buzzing around me and into the jungle. Small tree limbs fell to the ground from hits and more bullets ricocheted from rocks and metal objects. I didn't have any weapon with me—who would think this could ever happen here?

First combat area on my trip down the Ho Chi Minh trail, east of Nhang, Laos.

Back in Hanoi, I remember Major Vu, commanding officer of the first convey that left Hanoi discussing how drug gangs and smugglers could be a threat. These thugs could have been watching us, and when we couldn't fight back with force, they would attack. We had been depleting our personnel and suppliers coming down the trail to different assigned posts. Now, these thugs were at the camp trying to kill everyone.

My heart and mind raced with ideas on what to do to protect myself and others at the camp. I continued to get closer and closer to our campsite. The noise of war was loud with hollering and screaming, and this blurred my actions. I could hear other voices speaking a different language.

I listened for our armed North Vietnamese Army but I didn't know what condition they were in. Time was moving fast, and the small arms fire grew louder and louder as I came closer to the camp. My adrenaline rose higher and higher.

I could see NVA troops laying on the ground, not moving. Others moaned with severe pain. I didn't know how many were wounded. I wanted to help but I just couldn't run to them and give them aid. I crawled on my belly at the edge of the jungle, looking for a weapon to defend myself, but I didn't see anything that I could use. Thick smoke came from a truck hit by RPGs. Using the smoke as cover to move closer toward the troop truck, I saw a foxhole shovel laying on the ground to the left of its rear wheel.

The foxhole shovel used as my first weapon to save Major Vu from being stabbed with a bayonet.

I used an AK-47 in the first battle to illuminate any use of deathly force against me.

Handmade by my father, Mr. Wilson, and was used for deer hunting in Vermont. I used this knife in my first battle incident.

I can use this shovel to defend myself, I thought. I saw Major Vu on his knees—he was wounded in the chest and shoulder and leaned against a Russian jeep. As he tried to motion to me to stay away, a person dressed in native Montagnard clothing—a drug gang mercenary—came running toward me with a rifle and bayonet, ready to stab me on the right side of my chest.

I did not hesitate about what actions to take. I jumped up, howling a battle cry, and swung the foxhole shovel like a baseball bat, slicing his neck just above his shoulders, almost cutting his head off. Only the back of his neck skin held his head on the body.

His bloodied body fell to the ground, and I picked up his AK-47, checking it over. The magazine was empty. I looked to my left where Major Vu now lay on the ground, thankfully still alive, as another mercenary dressed in regional Montagnard clothing came at him with a bayonet. I rushed over, crying out with another battle cry. I overcame this thug and stabbed him in the chest then his throat. A gurgling noise escaped his larynx as blood made its way out of the body. I hastily kicked him off my bayonet and got ready to attack another.

All the while, I howled out battle cries. My adrenaline continued to rise, exploding with combat-aggressive readiness, as I ran toward another invader. Just before I went to stab him, he dropped his rifle and ran off into the jungle.

The combat activity around me stopped. Looking to my right, I saw a wounded mercenary slowly crawling toward one of our jeeps. I went to him and rolled him over onto his back. Taking my handmade hunting knife my father made for me, I made a surgical incision just below his stomach and, with my forefinger, located his small intestine and cut it off the stomach. Pulling about five feet out, I tied it to the bumper of the jeep.

I asked him if he could hear me. He started to shout "fuck you" repeatedly. I wanted him to crawl on his back down the hill pulling all the intestines out of his body. His voice grew weaker and weaker, and finally, it stopped.

I started to come down from the adrenaline high, and my heartbeat began to slow. I turned and walked over to a log where I sat down to get my bearings and think about what happened. I remembered looking the last invader in the eyes. I was unconcerned about him running away. I wanted to kill him. He was young looking, yet I didn't care what age he was.

I looked at my arms and clothing covered with blood. I checked myself to see if the blood was mine. I was relieved that most of the blood came from the invaders. I was cut on my arms, legs, and stomach, but not seriously. A little first aid would take care of my wounds.

Killing in combat situations was easy for me this morning. I went into a trance; everything was moving in slow motion, and I could hear other people crying out for help. But I didn't lose my focus to continue killing. I moved with such power and determination to kill and fight to stay alive. The people I killed that morning, as I thought back, had fathers and mothers and could have been married with families. I was thankful to God for letting me live this morning in hell. I didn't want to die in this backwater country.

I raised both arms toward the sky and shouted out, "Praise God! I love you." I was left with an appreciation for life. One must enjoy each day of their life, for at any moment, one's life could be shortened. I understood how quickly a life can end. I had taken three lives this morning but saved so many other lives in the camp.

The sky opened and rain came down to wash away the scars of war. I noticed in the madness, the blood of the fallen NVA troops and invading thugs slowly made a path down the small hill. Despite the rain, the sun was shining, a rainbow could be seen in the distance. The rain continued for approximately two hours, turning all the dirt areas into mud holes.

> **WHEN I THINK BACK TO THIS EXPERIENCE NEAR NHANG, LAOS, TWO SONGS BY CREEDENCE CLEARWATER REVIVAL COME TO MIND: "HAVE YOU EVER SEEN THE RAIN?" AND "WHO'LL STOP THE RAIN." THESE TWO SONGS GIVE ME FLASHBACKS AND MEMORIES OF THIS INCIDENT. I REMEMBER THAT, AS THE RAIN POURED DOWN, IT WASHED THE BLOOD FROM THE AREA. THE HARD DOWNPOUR MADE SMALL POOLS OF BLOOD AND WATER. WHEN THE POOL BEGAN TO FILL UP, THE DIRT WOULD BREAK AWAY THE SOIL AND RUN DOWN TO MAKE A LARGER POOL FARTHER ALONG THE GENTLE HILL. ONCE THE RAIN STOPPED, MOST OF THE EVIDENCE OF THE BATTLE WAS WASHED AWAY, AND I WONDER...**

The invaders had taken what they could—medical supplies, a few weapons, and bags of rice—then melted into the jungle.

I had three AK-47s from the invaders I had killed. Choosing the best one for my carry, I found three magazines along with a metal container full of ammunition. I loaded the magazines and put one in the AK-47 I kept. I wrapped the other two AK-47s with a hammock and put them in the Russian jeep as a remembrance of this day.

I looked around the battle area, hoping to find the foxhole shovel, and I searched for my things, which were almost buried in the mud and dirt near my sleeping area. I located the foxhole shovel and put it with the AK-47s in the jeep.

RPGs had come close to this area, causing a lot of damage. I checked the camera equipment and other gear. They were dirty and badly needed cleaning. My clothing was full of mud and dirt but it helped to protect the camera equipment from getting damaged. I lost one secret camera but I had one more. I searched everywhere for the secret camera but had no luck finding it.

After the smoke settled, only six of us had made it through this battle. The NVA troops that were left retrieved AK-47s, SKSs, and needed ammunition. They gathered up and reloaded the magazines just in case we got attacked again. NVAs that made it through with minor wounds helped each other with first aid. I gave myself first aid and helped others with medical care.

But Major Vu had lost too much blood and died. His troopers missed him. Lieutenant Minh, who was wounded in the leg, took command and called for additional troops to come and take care of the dead and help with medical care. We would be supplied with troops, weapons, and food, giving us needed support to get to Pak Nhai in Cambodia.

I walked around the campsite and looked at the destruction that the combat had brought to this camp. Lives were taken because a few people had the power to rule over ours. Selfishness, thirst for power coupled with money, and intimidation overshadowed human beings' rights to live here.

I took several rolls of photographs and recorded the area. Getting coverage for both sides of this incident, location, what we were doing there, how many troops were killed and wounded, and getting the invaders documented so someone could find out who these devil men were. I knew Major Vu's staff wanted all the recorded history of this incident. It was important for Nha Trang Headquarters to get this report as soon as possible. They would need this information for their reports back in Hanoi and would share it with the late Major Vu's family. Lieutenant Minh had a detail to get their comrades' bodies ready to be transported back to Hanoi.

I was feeling tired and badly needed to wash off the blood from my body, so I returned to my alligator friends' waterfall for another shower. However, this time, I brought my AK-47 with three extra magazines. I returned to the campsite to find some food waiting for me. The snake meal tasted good along with hot tea, fruit, and honey from the nearby jungle.

After we had the meal and cleared up the campsite the best we could, three trucks arrived with NVA troops and supplies. Major Tran was to be our replacement commander. We were headed toward Pak Nhai, closer to South Vietnam. I was glad to hear the news about going to Pak Nhai. I had a handler/asset[1] there to hand over vital information about the intel I gathered on this trip and our attack.

We loaded up and left for Pak Nhai. It could take us two days depending on the roads, weather, possible repairs on trucks, and other unknown delays. I sat in the back with the NVA troops and thought about the cooks' job back in Nha Trang that Lieutenant Colonel Miller offered me. *Too late now, I'm in the saddle here and not turning back.*

---

[1] **Handlers** are trained specialists in managing field agents and are with the intelligence agency. They provide the field agent with instructions, money, documents, special clothing, and camera equipment, and receive all intelligence gathering from the field agent. The **asset** is trained to give support to the handler and gather documents from the field agent and pass on any pertinent information to the handler. The asset also gives aid to the field agent.

I couldn't stop myself from thinking of Woodstock and what Sofie, my love back home, might be doing. No word from me in months; it seemed like a year had gone by. As I bounced around in the back of the truck, I remembered what my father told me back in Vermont: "Hunting for another human being is the greatest hunt of all." No truer words than these had been spoken in my experience so far on the path of life survival.

My waterfall shower

My friends at the waterfall pool

CHAPTER 2
GOING TO PAK NHAI

I heard from the new lead NVA officer Major Tran that "time was important to get to Pak Nhai to get the new tunnels completed before Têt.[2] We have new and faster-digging equipment to make trenches for the tunnels. These new machines could dig large areas for underground barracks, storage rooms, and medical rooms for surgery."

Major Tran was excited and wanted to get to Pak Nhai and see this new heavy-duty equipment perform.

A faster-digging equipment from Russia.

---

[2] *The name for the lunar new year celebration in Vietnam.*

On the Cambodian and Vietnam border, the Viet Cong tunnel complex went up into the stone mountain's underground headquarters. You can see the red line going across the field is the underground main road. The grass hasn't completely grown back but it was dug and finished three weeks ago. In the mountainside, the underground tunnel was dug by hand, using small diggers. Stones were replaced to cover the tunnel.

A water hole was used to camouflage the underground tunnel in this photo entry, and the exit to a small village warehouse is plain to see the tunnel path.

This information was very vital. Had to document and get it into a handler/asset(s) possession once to Pak Nhai. Something was going to happen during Tết. I had excellent intel on the main routes of the Ho Chi Minh Trail and all the secret roadways, waterways, underground storage locations, and tunnel locations. How do they build the tunnels quickly? How do they camouflage their construction sites so they wouldn't be seen from the air? By using track hoes and heavy equipment to dig the tunnels, underground housing, hospitals, and storage for military hardware, and using hundreds of people to cover the tunnels with thick planks to keep the tunnel's ceiling from falling in. Another group of workers covers the tunnels with dirt using small bulldozers and hand shovels. Hundreds more would come along planting trees and plants from the jungle to complete the coverage of the new construction. These trees and plants grow quickly in this environment. In just a few days, you couldn't tell there was a tunnel complex under your feet.

Going along the rough road, I dozed off and started to dream about being home with my family and Sofie. *Oh, home, it's so far away from here. I have been told about sixteen thousand miles to the East Coast.*

My thoughts drifted back to Sofie's inviting arms. We truly had a grand time together. In the few months of our relationship, we exchanged a true understanding of each other's feelings toward one another. It was very sad to pull away from her arms and catch the airplane in Boston.

As I looked back over the events that took me away from all the loving people in my life, the truck drove over rocks and around trees that had fallen into the narrow road. I woke up when the truck stopped, and we all got off.

It was time to drink water and go into the jungle to relieve ourselves. After walking around the small convoy and talking to three soldiers in

French, they told me I was a legend. Fighting with the mercenaries, killing them in hand-to-hand combat.

"You must have experience in the past. You know how to handle yourself. We are pleased to have you with us."

I was taken aback by their comments and expressed my sincerity to them. I thanked them for giving me the freedom to record all of their activities. I explained to them that writing and taking photographs was my mission, putting stories together with photos and having them printed back in France and Hanoi.

"I enjoy the free hand your country has given me to tell your story worldwide," I told them.

We then got back into the trucks and continued going to the Montagnard village. One of the NVA soldiers told me to get in the front seat. It is more comfortable and I would enjoy the ride. I accepted his gesture and got into the front seat. It was noisy and difficult to find a spot to continue my dream. Due to the rhythm of the truck's movements, I managed to pick up where I left off. In my new comfort zone, I must keep one eye open. Oh, I wanted to go back to my dream and relive the romantic times with Sofie. Speaking French, I asked the truck driver sitting beside me, "How far is it to our next stopping location?"

"A long ride yet," the truck driver replied, "maybe all-day driving and maybe into the night. I am hoping to get there just in time for a hot meal. We will be staying in Montagnard village for the night."

As the truck rumbled down the rough road, I found a comfortable spot in the corner of the cab. Supporting my back and shoulders, and with one eye open, I wandered back into the dream with Sofie. In the back of my mind, a little voice reminded me not to speak in English. This part of my dream was so real, I woke up to see if the truck driver was watching me. Could I have been speaking English? I would be killed at the next stop. I looked at the truck driver, trying to read his body language to get an idea of what I might have said. Nothing unusual came across his face. I continued to stay awake and be on guard with due diligence.

Finally, we arrived in the Montagnard village. The troop trucks stopped around the main entrance of the small village, and the driver left plenty of room for all the troop trucks to be spaced out for security precautions. It was a delicate moment to get out of the truck and walk around, stretching my body, especially my legs.

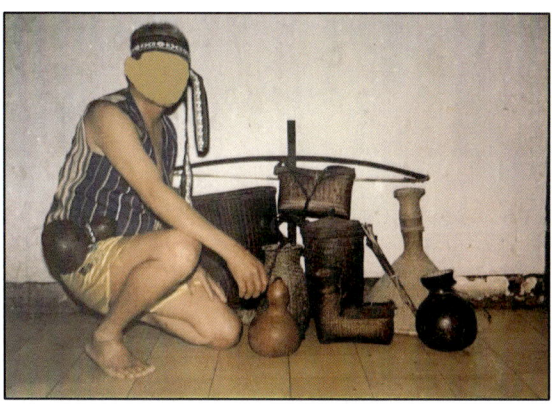

  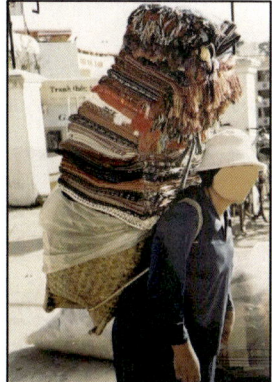

Montagnard villagers along the Ho Chi Minh trail in Laos and Cambodia.

Lieutenant Minh went to the last troop truck and grabbed a bag of rice. He also had an NVA soldier bring a case of thirty-three beers. This would be a hit with the villagers.

We gathered around the campfire, and the ladies in the village carried our meals for us. We were set apart from one another for general security reasons, with AK-47s at our sides, ready for any unexpected guests. We also had a small machine gun mounted in the bed of the first troop truck. The other village near Nhang, Laos, wasn't very friendly. They seemed to be friendly on the outside but felt different on the inside. This Montagnard village here appeared friendly and welcomed us.

The food was exceptional, or maybe I was very hungry. The meal consisted of brown snake, chicken, carrots, beets, mushrooms, and corn. You know I was hungry and the snake tasted surprisingly good. We washed down the food with coconut milk. Montagnard villagers pretended the food was out of this world. Well, it was out of this world.

All of us sang songs from that region. The villagers played their handmade bamboo musical instruments. The music these villagers played is like the flute music of the South American tribes. It was relaxing for all of us, but I couldn't stop thinking about Sofie and how she should experience this event.

After eating, Lieutenant Minh got a detail together to clean the area and help the villagers with anything they needed. We all helped with the cleaning detail, but sleep was a high priority. I found a place to hang my hammock and rest for the night.

The sun came up bright and shiny the next morning. I could hear the NVA troops talking about our last encounter at Nhang. All of us were alert and ready for any surprise action that may come out of the dense jungle. We took turns eating breakfast while others spread out to guard.

Some looked at me as if I could help them when attacked. If they only knew I was lucky before and could only fight for myself. Thankfully, the troops overall seemed strong and well-militarily trained.

We said farewell to our village friends and loaded into the troop trucks and headed for Pak Nhai, Cambodia.

CHAPTER 3
Beginning of My Story, Two Years Earlier

The journey started at the Woodstock Country Club golf course in Woodstock, Vermont, in the late fall afternoon. The air was crisp and fresh that Labor Day weekend in 1965. I had just returned from France, where I worked the summer months at a ski-manufacturing facility.

I was on the fourteenth hole when a thunderstorm started. I ran to a shelter nearby and waited for the storm to pass, when a young, attractive lady entered the shelter. She wore a lightweight white blouse—the type when wet, you can see everything. I noticed right away she wasn't wearing a bra, her breasts visible through the wet blouse. I must tell you that her breasts were firm and well above average in size. I tried to keep my eyes off her twins and look at her inviting eyes; I tried hard to focus on other issues that might be interesting to her.

"What is your name? Do you play golf often? What are some of your hobbies?" I asked.

She started with her name, "Sofie Solberg, from Bergen, Norway. I play golf often, as well as tennis. I ski, cycle, yacht, and enjoy listening to primitive flute music from the Indians in South America."

Sofie's accent was seductive to my ears. I replied to Sofie, "We have things in common. I am a professional ski instructor in America and teach at the ski resort here in Woodstock. During my college breaks, I teach skiing to guests at the inn or to other people who want ski lessons."

Sofie was pleased to hear this and wanted to know more about my history.

The rain had finally stopped, so we could leave the shelter.

"Would you like to join me for the remaining holes?" I asked Sofie, and she accepted my invitation.

Between holes, Sofie told me she moved from Norway, went to Boston for a short time, then moved to Woodstock recently.

"I liked the countryside, and Woodstock was attractive and quaint." Sofie said. "I stay with Mr. and Mrs. Steven Smith, friends of my parents, just outside the village. This area around Woodstock reminded me of a summer home my parents rented in Norway's countryside."

I let Sofie tee off first, and I noticed her nipples push her blouse outward during her golf swing. I couldn't stop thinking about her attractive athletic body and that she probably had several boyfriends courting her, or at least a boyfriend.

We played two holes, then Sofie said, "I need to stop playing. I am getting cold."

"I have a sweatshirt that would help keep you warm," I said. "I suggest that you remove your wet blouse." She went behind a tree and removed the wet blouse and put on the sweatshirt. Then she returned to the fairway, and we continued to play.

Finishing the course, I asked, "Sofie, would you enjoy having dinner with me at your favorite restaurant?"

"I have to go home and change into dry clothes," Sofie responded.

"I understand, and you should get out of those wet clothes," I replied. "You can return the sweatshirt at another time."

"Do you golf here often?" Sofie asked.

"I am a non-paying member here at the club," I explained to Sofie, "but working for the resort, I can play golf and tennis during the summer months." I went on to say, "I just returned from France the other day. This summer, I was working in a ski factory in Thonon-les-Bains. If you have time, I would like to tell the story."

"Of course," Sofie said. "I am very interested in knowing more about you."

"Let's go into the club and sit by the fireplace so you can start to get warm," I said.

Sofie agreed to go into the club and get warm by the fireplace.

"I met a man, Mr. Paul Pyix from France," I said. "He approached me after skiing during the Christmas holiday break and asked me if I would like to come to his ski factory in France and learn how to fabricate skis. He was planning on having a distribution center near Woodstock. He needed a person to set up and manage the center. He went on to say that his wife and he had been observing my skiing over the holiday period. They remarked that my skiing performance reminded them of a skilled ballerina."

I continued. "They enjoyed seeing me ski and thought others would agree. My skiing talent would be beneficial in demonstrating the products at different ski areas during the winter months, ski markets, ski shows, and managing the center. I became interested in his proposal and wanted to learn more about his plans and what he expected from me. Mr. Pyix went

John Wilson, seen here skiing in Vermont, is the inspiration for the character Jean Claude Martin.

on to ask me if I could join them for dinner. I replied that I could, and we met at Woodstock Inn at six p.m. that night."

Sofie interrupted me. "I want to hear about your experience in France. Also, can you join me for golf tomorrow and continue our conversation?"

"Of course," I said, "I can join you tomorrow. What time do you want to start? However, the caveat is, I would enjoy taking you out to dinner in the evening. Would you like that?"

"We will see how our golf scores add up at the end of eighteen holes," Sofie replied.

"Okay," I agreed. I thought that maybe I should let her win, or get close to winning. I would see how well I play tomorrow to see what strategy to use.

After our conversations, I kissed the back of her hand and she lit up like a Christmas tree. What a warm smile came across her face. Boy, oh, boy, her smile would melt a glacier. We parted for the evening with warm feelings toward each other. I offered to drive her home, but she had her vehicle.

That night, I imagined her petite model figure—her body shape, her buttocks, her wet see-through blouse with her nipples pushing outward as she swung the golf club, her skin like milk. In the rain, she was beautiful, and her long blonde hair draped over her shoulders.

We played golf the next day at ten a.m. We played the first nine holes, and both of us were on top of our game. Sofie was playing extremely well and was ahead of me by three strokes. She was very happy and rubbed it in.

"I come behind scorers," I explained to her. "Some players get tired on the last five holes, giving me the advantage, allowing me to win the game."

"Not a chance today, John," Sofie said.

We finished the course, and I must say, she did win the game by four strokes. I must have another game right away, like tomorrow.

"We have dinner tonight, right?" I asked.

"Only if you pay for dinner," Sofie replied.

"If I win tomorrow's game," I explained to Sofie, "we must play a third game to see who is the overall winner."

"I can't wait to find out who is better at golf—you or me," she said.

"Boy, you are tough and competitive," I said and went on to say that I liked this characteristic quality in a person.

"What time should I pick you up?" I asked.

"How far is the restaurant from Woodstock?" she asked.

"It's about thirty minutes," I said. "We can eat and later dance. There's great music and fun for all."

Sofie went to her home and got ready for the evening. We had a truly delightful evening together. When I walked her to her front porch at the end of the date, she turned and kissed me softly on my right cheek.

"What a lovely evening, John," Sofie said. "I want to have more of these special moments with you."

"We are playing golf tomorrow, right?" I immediately asked.

"Of course, and maybe a little tennis after the golf," Sofie replied.

"Great," I said, "I can't wait for you to chase my returns."

Sofie smiled. "Sure, John. I will see you tomorrow afternoon. Have a good night's rest for tomorrow; it will be challenging for both of us."

"Hey, Sofie, loser pays for dinner tomorrow night."

"Bring your wallet, John."

John Wilson at Woodstock Country Club.

CHAPTER 4
GETTING READY

At this time, I want to introduce myself, my name is John William Wilson. I was raised in a solid family residence, in the small town of Sharon, Vermont. When I went to high school, I played varsity soccer, basketball, and baseball.

I attended State College in the fall of 1963. I was a professional ski instructor working at the ski area in Woodstock. Skiing with other ski instructors from France gave me a window to learn French. Gaining experience with Mr. Paul Pyxis's employment in France improved my French-speaking abilities. These avenues gave me the best French language course. Having this exposure to different people and making friends with them and speaking French most of the time was my foundation for the French language. Also, Montreal, Canada, was close by for me to practice my French.

I enjoyed deer hunting with my father and brother. I would also go fishing at different locations around our home with my father. My father was also a professional trapper and would trap the following animals for their fur: mink, red foxes, beaver, raccoons, bobcats, fisher cats, weasel, and muskrats. He showed and taught me their habits, pointing out their strengths and weaknesses—how older bucks will watch their tracks from a higher location, looking down onto their trail left below for any predators.

Going back to Sofie, we continued to enjoy our steamy love companionship, playing golf, tennis, indoor tennis, skiing, dancing at the ski resort, and a winter sleigh ride under the moonlight. We did manage to weave all these activities in the first few months of our relationship. I wanted to invite Sofie to come and have dinner with my parents, but I hesitated to ask her. I was waiting for the right moment.

I remembered her talking about music from the primitive flutes of South America. In my collection, I had several albums of primitive flute music from South America as well as other places in the world. I decided I would invite her for dinner with my parents and show her the albums.

"Would you be interested in meeting my family and listening to my primitive flute music from South American Indians?" I asked Sofie.

"Yes, I would love to," Sofie replied very quickly.

That night, I asked Sofie, "Would you like to look over the albums?"

"Yes, I would," Sofie said. "John, these are the ones I was telling you about while playing golf."

We laughed together and continued to look at other albums of interest. My parents, Sofie, and I enjoyed listening to her album selections. Sofie displayed warmth in our home, and my parents reflected the same feelings. Sofie fit right into our family, like fingers into leather gloves.

Our relationship had been a delightful few months; however, there was a cloud hanging over my head. I started to get draft notices every three months from the local selective service board office. Naturally, I could get deferred for being in school. But I thought it was strange getting these notices frequently in the mail. Right up until I graduated from college.

John Wilson getting ready to leave.

CHAPTER 5
FORT BRAGG BOOGIE

Just two weeks after graduating, I received another notice in the mail to report for a physical in the spring of 1966. I passed the physical and moved on to a battery of testing. I decided if I was going to Vietnam, I was going to try to get a military occupational specialty (MOS) that I could use after military service. I did very well in my scores—strong in languages, mathematics, people skills, organizational skills, and photography.

After I finished testing, there was a short interview with the staff who were conducting the exams. There weren't any promises made by the army administration staff. However, their ending comments were that I had a good chance of getting into the intelligence branch as a combat photographer/intelligence gathering MOS.

On July 31, 1966, I received my instructions to report to Manchester by 07:00—I was headed to Fort Bragg, North Carolina, for basic training. The other men getting their physicals the same day as me were headed to Fort Drum in New York or Fort Dix in New Jersey. Why was I going to Fort Bragg, home of the 82nd Airborne and 5th Special Forces Group?

I invited Sofie to have dinner at my home in Sharon for the second time. She happily accepted the invitation. Sofie came early in the afternoon to spend more time with me and my family. Sofie went upstairs to see what I was doing while my mother went grocery shopping in another town. I was in the walk-in closet getting my clothing ready to pack. I came out and Sofie was completely undressed with her beautiful body standing by the bed with her left arm wrapped around the bedpost. The shaded sunlight coming into the room that touched her body made her look like a painted picture.

"You are so beautiful, gorgeous, and sexy," I said, "and I will never forget these moments which lie in my heart. I will take you wherever I go."

"John, throughout the relationship you have been a gentleman," Sofie replied. "Not once have you made unwanted advancements toward me. You are a very sweet and loving person."

Sofie went on to say, "Before you go to Vietnam, I wanted to give you a gift that will last while you are gone from my side. John, your body is so hard and strong. I will keep you in my heart and mentally massage you. You can close your eyes and I will be there with you."

"I never had a romantic sexual relationship before," I replied.

"John, over these months, you and I have experienced sexual moments with each other." Sofie lovingly stated. "You know what makes me have multiple orgasms, I enjoy my role with you. Your explosive, rapid, pleasurable releases get me excitingly wet."

She then said, "Come to me and lay down beside me. Touch me tenderly all over my body and open your love gift and make love to me!"

This strong exchange of passion lasted several hours. We could hear my mother downstairs preparing dinner. Finally, Sofie and I took a long shower together. We played around while getting dressed, like two little kids taking clothes from one another, pillow fighting, and acting silly. When we settled down and were dressed, we went downstairs to help with dinner. I remember Sofie's blouse was buttoned incorrectly. I pointed this out to Sofie, and she smiled back at me. Sofie rebuttoned her blouse in another room and returned smiling.

All of us had a grand time together that evening, playing cards, listening to music, and visiting with each other. It was getting late, and my parents suggested that Sofie stay overnight. This was an easy decision to make. When my parents went to bed, Sofie and I hooked up for the night. All night we were glued together, and we didn't sleep at all.

"Don't leave; I want you to stay with me all night," Sofie said in her low sexy voice. "John, I didn't know making love with you would be so wonderful. What a memorable experience I am having with you before you leave for Vietnam."

"This is my gift to you, my love," I said to Sofie. "All the loveable togetherness we shared will be harbored in my heart and mind. I want these times to be fresh in my mind to carry me through the experience that lies ahead of me. I look forward to continuing our romance when I return home. I hope and pray our love will be a continuance of our past. We can start to move our relationship further ahead and spend time together without worrying about Vietnam."

It left me on cloud nine thinking about Sofie. I hoped all the time while in military service she would be there when I returned from Vietnam safely.

Sofie took me to Manchester to catch the bus going to Boston, then I would get a train to Fort Bragg, North Carolina. Leaving my parents in the morning was very emotional for all of us. I wished over and over that it would never come, but it did. Mentally, I was ready to get this over with and return to Sofie's arms once again. If it was meant to be, she would be ready for my return home.

Before I got on the bus, Sofie held me passionately, tight to her body, and kissed me—a kiss that would last for months to come. It was difficult to let go and say, "I'll see you soon." I expressed my sincere affection for her, telling her repeatedly that I would carry her in my heart, dream about her, and make love to her in my sleep.

As the bus door closed, I made it to my seat and called out to her through my bus window. "I love you forever, my darling Sofie!"

CHAPTER 6
TRAIN RIDE TO FORT BRAGG

It was a long train ride from Boston to Fort Bragg, North Carolina. While on the way, I was continuously thinking about home, Sofie, and skiing. These thoughts gave me the strength to move forward in this environment.

I made it through the eight weeks of basic training. But then, I had to go to Fort Monmouth, New Jersey, for more military schooling in combat photography as well as anatomy and physiology of the North Vietnamese Army (NVA) and Viet Cong men and ladies. I had high-level training in martial arts and different ways to kill a human in three seconds or less. I was at Fort Monmouth for seven months, sharpening my skills for a Vietnam tour.

In April 1967, I got to go home for thirty days before going to Vietnam. Sofie came down to New Jersey to pick me up. We didn't make it back to Vermont that day. We just about made it to the nearest hotel. It was exciting, comforting, to see Sofie again.

"It was hard waiting for you, and I am so happy to be back in your arms," Sofie whispered in my ear.

I could tell Sofie still had strong feelings toward me. We stayed in bed all day and all night. I remembered the warm spots on her body, the tender areas that gave Sofie pleasure. What an exciting time for both of us.

The next morning, we tried to get ready and head to Vermont, but we ended up on top of the sheets again. We couldn't stop hugging each other and exchanging passionate kisses. This gentle touching and caressing together started something new with Sofie and me. We were delayed by a few hours and hungry. We found a suitable restaurant along the way that would serve us breakfast. Then we were ready to head to Sharon, Vermont.

We arrived in time to be with my parents and have a special dinner with them. My mother went out of her way to have lobsters from Maine. It was a treat for all of us. My parents overloaded us with questions and were interested in what plans we might have for our future.

"Mother," I said, "we just came from a long drive and want to enjoy your company and eat this delicious meal. We can reply to all your questions later."

After dinner, all of us chipped in and did the dishes and cleaned the table. Finally, I thanked my parents for the homecoming welcome, and Sofie and I drove to Woodstock.

When we arrived at Sofie's cottage, there was a message from Mrs. Smith. It was an invitation to meet the Smiths on Saturday night for dinner. Sofie planned on cooking the dinner and I helped bring the food to the table. It was enlightening for me to share the evening with the Smiths. They were in the oil business, delivering heating fuel, gasoline, and kerosene in the Woodstock area for many years.

I volunteered to help with the dishes but was lured away to the living room with Mr. Richard Smith. He asked me questions about the military, and what my MOS was.

I brushed him off by saying, "I probably will find out later when I get to Vietnam."

"Going to Fort Bragg is a far cry from going to basic training at forts in the northeast," Mr. Richard Smith said.

"Yes," I replied. "If you have a chance, ask Sofie—she can give you any updates about my training at Fort Bragg."

The evening with the Smiths was cordial, and Sofie was pleased about the success. However, Mr. Smith was distant with me, but Mrs. Smith was warm and friendly. I thanked Sofie for the tasty dinner, saying how I looked forward to a lifetime of meals with her.

She laughed and said, "Me too."

Sofie took me home to Sharon that evening. Along the way, we stopped beside the road and talked about what we could do after I returned from Vietnam. It was interesting to hear what Sofie told me. She started by explaining why she was in Woodstock. Mr. Richard Smith was a customer of her father's in Norway. Mr. and Mrs. Smith had traveled to Bergen many times over the years and stayed with her parents. Her father, Bjorn Sorberg, supplied the fuel products and shipped them to the Boston port, while Mr. Smith loaded his trucks and came to Woodstock.

"I wanted to travel to the United States and see what it was like," Sofie said. "Mr. and Mrs. Smith volunteered their small cottage behind their house where I could stay, and my parents agreed with the plan. I came to Woodstock not knowing I would meet a character like you. It's God's wish for me to come here, and meeting you is a gift from God. I have read books about romances and having love affairs. John, I couldn't have met a nicer person than you. I love you!"

The Smiths were very protective and attentive to Sofie as if she was their daughter. I liked their stand on responsibility with Sofie. It made me feel good that the Smiths had this attitude toward Sofie. While I was gone, I would know that Sofie had the caring people she was living with. It was comforting to know.

We made it to Sharon, and my parents were asleep. Sofie and I went upstairs, stepping lightly. We took showers and laid down on the bed, looking out the window at the stars shining in the sky.

"I appreciate the evening with the Smiths and hearing how you got to Woodstock," I told Sofie. "I feel good about you living with them while I am gone from your side. I believe the Smiths will take good care of you and you'll have a comfortable place to stay, and you can go to my parents anytime you want to. You have captured their love and friendship. My mother would enjoy your company. Please visit them."

The next morning after breakfast, Sofie made a picnic to take on a trail walk together. Along the trail, I pointed out where the deer ran through the woods, making trails called "deer runways." I also showed her other animal habitats and how they survive the hard winter months. We found a location to spread the blanket and have our picnic near a waterfall.

"Being around you is like being with Daniel Boone," Sofie jokingly said.

Sofie and I made it home before the rain started, just in time to help my mother prepare dinner. After dinner, Sofie and I went to Hanover, New Hampshire, to see a movie. After, we came back home and went upstairs. I wanted to introduce her to more of my music. I started with Kitaro's "Silk Road," Leonard Cohen's "Suzanne," "La Flute Indienne," "The Indios flute through the Centuries," and the gypsy flute. When we finished listening to the albums, the sun was coming over the mountain, and downstairs my parents were moving about. I think to this day, they were making noise just for us.

We got dressed and went to join them for breakfast. My mother went out of her way for us, having made pancakes, bacon, fried eggs, and hot tea with honey.

Sofie's eyes grew wide in enjoyment—as if she was saying *wow* with her eyes.

My father asked if we could have a few moments in private after finishing breakfast.

"Of course," I said.

He started with the subject of my relationship with Sofie, going to Vietnam and leaving her here. "I am going to tell Sofie that she can come and visit us anytime she wants to, stay overnight if she is inclined to do so," he offered. "She means a lot to you, and we enjoy her company. We will pray for your safe return. This is a war you are stepping into—it will be dangerous. It's not a movie, but a real-life war. You haven't told us what you might be getting into in Vietnam, and I don't want to know. Use your hunting skills—you are an excellent shot with your deer rifle. Your mother will be sick not knowing your whereabouts. May God be with you and keep you safe. We love you, son!"

Afterward, Sofie wanted to know about my conversation with my father.

"He invited you to come and visit them anytime you want and stay overnight if you wish," I told Sofie.

Sofie was open to this idea and asked me, "Could I stay in your bedroom and dream about the romantic times we have shared?"

"Sofie, you don't have to ask. My love for you is real," I replied. "From the beginning, I was in love with you. It was hard for me to hold back my affection—I was burning inside, and I didn't want to scare you away. When I go to bed, I dream of you in my sleep. These dreams of us will be carried in my heart and mind while in Vietnam."

Love has a burning grip on my heart and mind. Sofie and I had a wonderful, unbelievable, warm, passionate exchange of love that day. These moments with Sofie would lighten my first year in Vietnam. Sofie was my hope and passion to return home. To hold her close to my body, touch her tenderly, and whisper my feelings into her ear.

The thirty-day leave was almost up. I didn't want to go to Vietnam but to go to Canada with Sofie. We spent time upstairs in my bedroom listening to our favorite albums. Sofie wrapped her long legs around my waist and held me close to her as we exchanged kisses.

"I want you forever, John," she whispered in my ear. "You are exciting to me when we are united. Having you close puts me in a trance. You are so talented and lovable."

CHAPTER 7
GOING TO 'NAM, JUNE 1967

The next morning, after my mother's tasty breakfast, Sofie and I left to go to the Boston International Airport, where I would then head to Oakland, California. I was left with a lasting expression on Sofie's face.

The loving memories we shared were written on her beautiful face. Alligator tears rolled down her face. I couldn't stand looking at her, but her loving touches smothered me.

My flight to California was blurry. I woke up while landing at the San Francisco International Airport. God, I felt so lonely.

I met my sister and brother-in-law with their family of three sweet girls at the gate. I had a two-day stay with them before reporting to the Oakland Transport Depot, located at the port authority. I made my way to a telephone and called my parents. In the past, I would say, at the end of our conversation, "See you soon," but that day, I said, "Good-bye." I couldn't call Sofie; it was too hard leaving her in Boston. I couldn't stand the frustration of speaking to her over the phone.

As I traveled toward Vietnam, there were more and more Green Berets on my flights. I stopped in Honolulu for a few hours, Guam, Manila, and Clark Air Force Base in the Philippines. At Clark Air Base, we stayed overnight, and the next morning, we headed to Pleiku, Vietnam. Most passengers wore the Green Beret on this flight. The Special Forces personnel had been to Vietnam before and were going back for another tour.

The flight was about halfway to Pleiku, and our plane was ordered to return to Clark Air Base. Pleiku was under attack and couldn't land there that day. The next morning, we were cleared to take off for Pleiku.

I remember landing in Pleiku on the perforated steel plating (PSP). They used PSP for runways in Vietnam. The sections were two feet wide by eight feet long and had interlocking areas at the ends and sides to hold the sections in place. When our plane landed on the PSP, plus when it reversed the props, the noise was loud and foreign to me. The first thing that came to my mind was, *We're going to crash-land.* Watching others on the flight, I could tell this landing was normal, so I stopped thinking about a crash landing and tried to relax.

Perforated steel plating. Pleiku, 1967

As we disembarked from the plane and waited for our duffel bags, a column of tanks passed by. The red dust of Pleiku went all over us.

"Welcome to Pleiku, Vietnam, gentlemen!" a seasoned Green Beret hollered out.

All of us reported, according to our last name. With mine beginning with a *W*, I had to wait a while. It was getting late in the evening, and I had nothing to eat, only what was served on the flight hours ago. Finally, it was my turn to check in. I was told I would be going to An Khê, home of the 1st Air Cavalry, after breakfast tomorrow. At the chow line, I investigated a kettle of milk and saw flies the size of my thumb. No breakfast for me.

I was then told my flight to An Khê was delayed until further notice. I spent my time walking around Pleiku and seeing what I could, but most of Pleiku was off-limits to me. I had two meals that day, and in the late evening, around 22:00, two other men and I were off to An Khê. We had three other passengers with us, but they were laying horizontally in bags at the bottom of the C-130 aircraft.

Again, the noise of landing on the PSP and reversing the props was strange to my ears. The three horizontal body bags moved forward from the reverse props' force of stopping the plane.

The back of the C-130 opened, and as we disembarked, there was nobody around and it was pitch-black. We didn't have any weapons and, oh boy, I hoped Charlie wasn't hiding in the jungle.

Way in the distance we could see two small lights coming. They looked like flashlights. Once again, I hoped it was friendly and not Charlie. As the lights came closer to us, I could see that it was a jeep. We loaded on the jeep and went to headquarters camp, where we were assigned a cot for that night.

The next morning, around 06:00, my name was announced over the PA system to report to Captain Massey in the headquarters company. Captain Massey came out of his tent office, and his mustache looked like water buffalo horns. I had never seen a mustache that large before. He asked me if I was John Wilson, and I showed him my orders. He went back into his office, and I followed. Captain Massey looked over my orders and explained to me that I was to report to the I Field Force Victory Headquarters in Nha Trang.

"Will you be ready in twenty minutes?" Captain Massey asked me.

"I was born ready, sir," I replied.

He came back saying, "I like that, Wilson. I might keep you around here."

I was transported to the airstrip by jeep. The helicopter (Huey) was ready for my trip to Nha Trang—with no bodies on board.

Helicopter trip from An Khê to Nha Trang.

Ariel views from An Khê, 1967.

Nha Trang Airport, 1967.

My eyes were wide open as I looked down and saw the different terrain, small villages, our ground forces on patrol, small hills cleared off from jungle vegetation, campsites with underground bunkers, and PSP-reinforced trenches going into large, fortified bunkers.

What a reality shock.

CHAPTER 8
NHA TRANG AIRPORT HEADQUARTERS

Airport at Nha Trang, 1967.

The temperature was warm, but having the doors open on the helicopter made the wind pleasantly cool. The flight was about forty-five minutes long to Nha Trang Airport. Yes, Nha Trang had an airport. A nice modern facility with tile bathrooms, toilets, and hot and cold running water with showers. I hadn't taken a shower in three days, and the Pleiku dust was still on me.

I secured my duffle bag and went to the bathroom to take a very long hot shower and put on clean clothes. From there, I moved to the cafeteria and had some food to eat. It wasn't my mother's cooking, but based on where I was today, it tasted delicious. Once I finished eating, I called for transportation to the I Field Force Victory Headquarters. Within thirty minutes, a jeep came and took me to the headquarters office to report.

It was late afternoon when I arrived, and nobody was around to check me in. My room was in an adjacent one-story concrete building. Outside my window were four tennis courts. Across the street was a beach with white sand. The Pacific Ocean is a beautiful beach with clear water. There were restaurants inside this compound; movies were shown nightly. There were seven bedrooms and four bathrooms at the end of the hall. What more could I want?

The hotel was very large, named the Grand Hotel during the French Indochina era. Now, it was made into the I Field Force Victory Headquarters in Nha Trang.

I Field Force Victory Headquarters, Nha Trang, 1967.

My heart cried out to hear Sofie's voice. I made my way to the telephone building, which was full of phone booths. I asked if I could make a phone call and the sergeant pointed to an empty booth.

I called Sofie, and she answered and started to cry.

I couldn't help myself from crying too. "I truly miss your loving feelings for me. I am so alone over here. I am looking forward to coming home and being in your arms and enjoying ourselves like old times."

"John, my life has stopped ever since you've been gone from my side," Sofie said. "Oh, John, I miss you terribly. I can't help crying."

"I don't know when I can call again," I replied. "Please stay in touch with my parents. It could be months before I have a chance to call. Please don't think anything has happened to me. I will always have you in my thoughts, Sofie. I dream of us together while I am sleeping. It is very real. Please stop crying. I love you; I love you. I must hang up now. Please write to me at the address I gave you! Your words of love are heartwarming. I will contact you at the first chance I have. Love you, see you soon!"

CHAPTER 9
MEETING WITH LIEUTENANT COLONEL STEVE MILLER

The next morning, I had breakfast with the personnel at the non-commissioned officer's cafeteria adjacent to the Grand Hotel. I would be working with and sharing a life with some of the people in this room over the next twelve months. I introduced myself and wanted to get to know everyone.

Lieutenant Colonel Steve Miller came over to my table and sat down. "Are you, Wilson, John W.?"

Lieutenant Colonel Steve Miller had a serious look and his eyes were deep with secrets. He was tall and slender, but not muscular. He reminded me of an administrator, with glasses on his face and a folder full of documents.

"Yes, I am, sir," I said.

"So, *you* are the chosen one. I was expecting someone smaller. I've been waiting for you to arrive," he said.

"I came in-country via Pleiku, was transported to An Khê, and arrived here yesterday," I explained. "I had a grand tour by helicopter of the central highlands."

"What you saw by air is just a sampling of your future," Lieutenant Colonel Miller replied. "Your home on the ground will be widened by three other countries while you are with us. My staff will process you—it'll take about four or five days. Once that is completed, you will travel to Bangkok, Thailand, and catch a commercial flight to Geneva, Switzerland. Colonel David Winter will meet you at the airport. He will transport you to Thonon-les-Bains, France. He'll be dressed in civilian clothing—address him as 'Mr. Winter.' Colonel Winter will instruct you about the special training you will attend. It will take about eight to nine weeks to complete all the phases of training. This will depend on your skills and how you perform. There will be many areas I haven't covered, but this training period has a high rate of failures. At this time, you will be number twenty-nine attending training in France."

Lieutenant Colonel Miller continued. "If you don't make the grade then you will be sent back to Nha Trang, probably assigned to the G-2 section or assigned to my staff. If you complete this course successfully, you will return to Hanoi from France. My staff will go over all the details with you. Instructions and funds will be available from your handlers *only*. All French contacts you have must be rekindled. While in France, you will be issued clothing made in France—two sets of used French Army fatigues, special socks, headgear, and combat boots. Nothing you have will connect you to US military forces.

"You will be issued a French passport with traveled places stamped inside the passport, making it look realistic. I understand you've lived in Thonon-les-Bains—this will be your hometown. Because you were born at the end of World War II, your parents moved across the lake and resided in Lausanne, Switzerland. After the war ended and Europe was busy getting back on its feet, your parents moved back to Thonon-les-Bains. You were a baby and wouldn't know anything about Lausanne. In Thonon-les-Bains, you must remember all the shops, restaurants, cafes, and all entertainment places. This status will illuminate anyone from accusing you of aiding and abetting the enemy. You are a French war correspondent, and your name is now "Jean Claude Martin." Your employer is the newspaper *La Combat-Haute-Savoie.* From now on, you mustn't tell anyone your real identity—*no one!* When you finish this assignment and come through this office returning to the States, you will be sworn back into the military service. You cannot communicate, send photos, or write to your parents and friends about what you are doing here in Vietnam."

"You are telling me that I can't tell my love, Sofie—who will be waiting for any information from me, anxious to hear my voice and be in her arms—anything about what I'm doing in Vietnam?" I said.

"Jean Claude, don't tell her anything about what and where you go in Vietnam," Lieutenant Colonel Miller replied. "If you complete your training, you will be working undercover. Is this crystal clear?"

"Yes, sir."

"Only speak French around us. If you speak English on assignment in Southeast Asia, you will be killed. We have a cook position opening at the headquarters company at the hotel in five days, we can transfer your MOS for that position. This will be the last chance you have before leaving for France for the advance training."

I just looked at him. "*Non, merci.*"

Jean Claude looking over documents from Lieutenant Colonel Miller.

"You are dismissed," Lieutenant Colonel Miller said. "Take time for yourself and think about what we discussed. Your room here will be saved for your rest and recuperation and you can place any valuables, IDs, and pictures of friends in there."

Lieutenant Colonel Miller continued. "Find cover for yourself, where you will be safest in another country, such as Laos or Cambodia. We have handlers and assets already in place that can be trusted and help you. Once you get some experience and exposure to these missions, you'll be just fine. In addition to what has been talked about between us today, you can have two days off to get ready for your trip to France. Just report to my staff what you are doing and when you would like to travel."

I replied to Lieutenant Colonel Miller in French. "I will report to your staff all my activities before leaving for France.

"You will fit in perfectly," Lieutenant Colonel Miller said. "I will introduce you to the commanding general before you leave for France. You must speak French with him. Pretend he is a North Vietnamese general you are meeting, and you want an interview for a newspaper article. The general will be impressed with your demeanor."

Lieutenant Colonel Miller continued. "Once you get to Geneva, you will be taken to another location twenty miles from the airport. You'll meet an asset, a female, and travel by vehicle to Thonon-les-Bains. You will have time to take photos of people you know and places of interest, relearn all the stores and what they sell. Your most important meeting will be with *La Combat-Haute-Savoie*. This newspaper will print your news articles and send them to you in Hanoi."

Lieutenant Colonel Miller went on. "Your contact at the newspaper is Mr. Valentine Gaudin. You will spend a few days with him and his family."

Lieutenant Colonel Miller moved forward. "Once you land in Hanoi and get through customs, expect to be delayed. They will go over your luggage with a fine-tooth comb. They will ask you to take off your clothing, open up your cameras, and check everything you brought with you. Colonel Winter in Geneva will give you used camera equipment. I suggest you purchase an old backpack. Travel light!"

Lieutenant Colonel Miller didn't pause. "After you are permitted to travel as a French war correspondent, the authorities will stamp your passport and give you a press ID, which permits you to travel with their troops, visiting interesting locations that are very important to our intelligence branch. Also, Jean Claude, you can return to France from Hanoi once or twice during your assignment period. If needed, go to the French Embassy and arrange your travel plans. Use these travel vendors wisely. If you go to France, only stay there for two weeks, then return to Hanoi immediately. After being in Vietnam for six months, you can stay in France for three weeks. You should have this time to relax around Thonon-les-Bains. You can restock your needs while in France. Colonel Winter will meet you at the airport the same way as before. Your escorts will be watching you and possibly taking you to the airport in Hanoi."

"Lieutenant Colonel Miller, can I meet friends in Europe?" I asked in French. "Can I travel to other countries in Europe? I know someone who has a small chalet at the end of the Chamonix Valley—only a few residents live there. I will know if strangers are in this hamlet by my friends who live there year-round."

"Yes, you can visit Chamonix while on your short leave," Lieutenant Colonel Miller responded in French. "You *cannot* travel to other countries in Europe. If you did, you would be out of our jurisdiction. We have a network of handlers in Geneva. The village in the Chamonix Valley sounds like a great place to rest. However, your handler *must* know where you are going, when you are returning to Geneva, and when you are leaving for Hanoi. Your handler needs to know who might be accompanying you in advance. The office in Geneva will check this person out for security reasons. Keep a record of your expenses. Keep a separate record of your travel costs. Colonel Winter can arrange a small rental vehicle to use during this period. If you can accept these conditions, you have permission."

Still speaking French, I replied, "I do agree to these conditions and will be responsible to everyone who is watching out for me. I appreciate this opportunity to serve my country."

Lieutenant Colonel Miller dismissed me, giving me time for the rest of the day for myself.

I had another chance to telephone Sofie before leaving for Geneva, Switzerland. The gravity to do so pulled me and my heart cried out to hear Sofie's voice again. I rushed to the telephone building and found an empty booth. I called Sofie, but she didn't answer. I couldn't help myself from crying inside. I returned two hours later but she was still away from her phone. I left a recording on her machine that I called and that I didn't know when I could call her again.

"Don't be saddened by this," I said. "I will try again just as soon as I can. I love you, my darling Sofie."

I tried resting but I couldn't due to the slight chance I could arrange a get-together in Geneva with her. It was late in the evening, and I planned to call one more time to see if Sofie was home. The phone rang several times before she answered. She was surprised, and I was extremely happy she was home. I wanted to tell her we could meet in Geneva. I wanted to explain to her that military staff could be listening to our conversation. I knew she had a current passport. I thought that I could reimburse the airline ticket and other expenses she might have for this trip. I could contact an old skiing friend that has a small ski chalet in Le Tour, France, a very small skiing village and, during off-ski season, a magnet for mountain climbers.

Naturally, I couldn't tell her anything about my wishful dream of meeting her in Geneva and driving up to Le Tour, France. However, we had a warm conversation over the phone. It was very difficult for us to say "See you soon." What a memorable phone call, giving each other hope of another phone call soon. My time was up for this phone call, and now I could get a good night's sleep.

CHAPTER 10
TRAINING IN FRANCE

The next morning after breakfast, I had another meeting with Lieutenant Colonel Miller.

"Remember always," Lieutenant Colonel Miller began, "your escorts will be spies. More than likely, they will assign an attractive female to be with you. In your case, a male spy will be close by. Ask to visit the battle site of Dien Bien Phu—the bloodiest and most devastating battle to the French Union in 1954. Once you have a chance to look around, take pictures and get some interviews from the natives who might have seen the battle and see about making arrangements to travel south. Our handlers and assets will be incognito but noticeable to you. Be careful not to expose them. My staff will share with you the details of exchanging intelligence while in the field. However, all photos and stories about NVA and Viet Cong personnel must go through the leader you are assigned to. They will look at your material and decide what can be printed. Contact our handlers and assets in Hanoi so you can make drop-offs and arrange trips into Laos and Cambodia. Learn the code my staff will give you. Leave information at secret locations set up by the handlers and assets. Later, you will have a say about the importance of intelligence gathering and learn to manage your assets in the field. First, you must understand how we pass on top-secret information. It is different from what you have been taught back at Fort Monmouth because we have you act out real scenarios and enactments, not from lectures like at Fort Monmouth."

"Gee, thank you for telling me," I replied in French.

Lieutenant Colonel Miller continued. "If you have any questions about anything come to me or my staff for answers. Best to be prepared about what to expect in Hanoi airport today."

"I will go over the material thoroughly and make notes of what was discussed in our meetings," I said in French. "If I have questions I will go to your staff for clarity."

I left Lieutenant Colonel Miller's office and returned to my quarters to review the mission that lay ahead of me. It was a lot for a Vermont country boy like me. I ate supper and then went to bed early that evening.

In the morning, I was on my way to Bangkok International Airport on the first leg of my trip to France. I packed my luggage and was ready to leave in the morning at 08:00. Traveling to Bangkok, Thailand, on an old military airplane was interesting. Luckily, we made it, and I was relieved to walk on the ground. I made it to the terminal, checked in, and got my seat assignment. Once I was on the plane after a three-hour wait, the flight was enjoyable and I had a good time along the way, even talking to a few passengers in French for the first time. This gave me a chance to help them out with their travel plans. I had several inexpensive hotels to suggest. The big challenge was my chance to *constantly* speak French. I couldn't slip up in my relaxed mood.

I am Jean Claude Martin from Thonon-les-Bains, France.

Having several people on the flight to have conversations with helped the time go by. Soon we landed at Geneva International Airport.

Sure enough, there was a vehicle parked on the top floor of the parking lot as instructed by Lieutenant Colonel Miller. Only a few vehicles were parked in this location, making it easy to spot. I didn't have to introduce myself to the handler, David Winter, who had my file with photos.

David Winter approached me with a very stern look about him. Dressed incognito with movements that seemed to be looking for something or anything suspicious in our surroundings, his introduction was cold. I felt concerned about my first contact with him.

We drove to the next location outside Geneva and picked up a female asset, Ms. Teresa Monet. She had a warmer personality, was attractive, and had some human relationships with ordinary people. From here I traveled to Thonon-les-Bains.

"I have most of the locations I can take you to purchase your items," my handler, Colonel David Winter, said. "However, you will have time to shop after you complete your training and fulfill all the requirements of a combat journalist. You will have a difficult schedule and a very demanding physical, as well as classroom lectures, and you will compete with others for this MOS slot. Thirty applicants have different language skills, but all of them can go to Vietnam and report back to our intelligence agencies. It's not a picnic, Martin."

Colonel Winter went on to say, "We'll need some time to drive to our supply house outside Thonon-les-Bains later this afternoon. There, you will be issued old-looking fatigues, used combat boots, a handgun, a knife, and a beat-up backpack along with cameras with secret equipment and other required equipment for this training. I know a quaint small place for dinner nearby."

After our errands, and ordering our meal, I thought this would be a good time for me to express my appreciation.

I started by saying, "My trip to France is exciting, to say the least.

Going to different places to get my equipment and different identification documents refreshed the locations in my memory. Colonel Winter, I will have my work cut out for me at your training center."

"Would you give me some advice before I leave on my Vietnam vacation?" I asked Colonel Winter.

"Of course," Colonel Winter replied. "I am glad to share with you my experiences while in Vietnam. Be careful! Don't trust any people you meet outside the circle of handlers and assets. Seek places you can be safe during the night. Getting rest, eating healthy food, and having good health is the top priority. Yes, your mission is important but being alive is the pinnacle in the overall scheme of the mission. I have several pairs of real silver chopsticks.

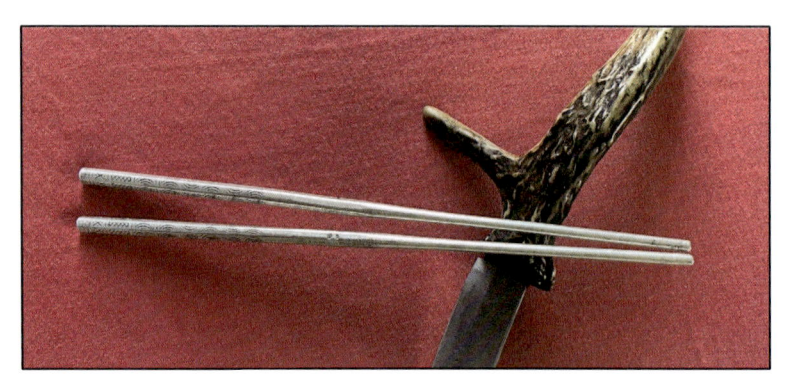

Colonel Winter's real silver chopsticks—if the food was poisoned, the tips would turn black.

"I'll give you one set to take with you. If your food is poisoned, about one inch of the chopstick end will turn black," Colonel Winter continued to explain. "In China, the dynasties and important families would use silver chopsticks to test their meals. Be aware of what is going on around you and be alert. Don't be too fast passing on intel to your handlers and assets, for they could have spies watching them and you would be endangering them and yourself."

"Before coming to France," I said, "my meeting with Lieutenant Colonel Miller told me about a cook leaving Nha Trang in a few days. I could replace him if I wanted to. Maybe I should have taken Lieutenant Colonel Miller's offer . . ."

"I salute you for your courage," Colonel Winter said. "Handling dangerous situations and developing all the affirmations successfully will be quite an experience for you. It's time to go and get ready for a big day tomorrow," Colonel Winter stated. "You have important engagements to make and you should get ready for your training. Get prepared for the identification process in the morning, which could take several hours."

I was up early the next morning and embraced the sun shining into the outside breakfast area. It was a quiet morning—birds were busy flying around the blooming flowers. I had just finished my meal when Colonel Winter and Ms. Monet arrived to take me for the morning engagements.

"Good morning, Jean Claude," Colonel Winter stated, "I hope you had a restful night. You have been instructed by Lieutenant Colonel Miller in Nha Trang about the program here in France. All your processing is very important and one of the most interesting ones will start today right after you receive your equipment and clothing. You will begin with the physical training phase, then the psychological phase includes waterboarding and other related training, along with the firing range. Once your performance is successful with these tests, our staff have other phases you must complete satisfactorily. This process will take a total of eight weeks or more to complete. If your performance has high scores, you will receive your new IDs. Then you will have an interview."

"What kind of an interview?" I asked.

"You'll take a polygraph; that is the last phase," Colonel Winter said. "It is a standard procedure for an individual who is assigned an MOS of combat war correspondent. Nothing to think about—you will do fine, Jean Claude."

I was able to pass the polygraph, physical training, and firing ranges—all with high marks. The changes with my nationality and becoming a Frenchman were completed. I had just two days left to shop to find things I would need for my job in Vietnam.

I met with the principals of the newspaper *La Combat-Haute-Savoie* and introduced myself and reviewed my role while covering the war in Southeast Asia. I explained that I would be sending them newspaper articles and pictures of the war in Vietnam and other conflicts in the region. I received a file with all the details for sending them my material to be printed. My stories would appear in a special newspaper that would highlight my coverage. Everything would be shipped air express to the French Embassy in Hanoi, then later handed over to the military intelligence command of North Vietnam.

All my identifications would also be shipped air express to the news bureau in Hanoi, introducing me as one of their correspondents. They gave me a press identification badge to have while entering the Hanoi International Airport Security authorities.

CHAPTER 11

HANOI

Finally, it was showtime. The next morning, I was off to Hanoi, North Vietnam. The reality was setting in, and I became ill just thinking about what lay ahead. I would have to check in with the North Vietnam authorities at the airport passport station. Police officers would ask questions about what was bringing me to Hanoi. I couldn't get nervous; I needed to stay focused on my mission—and I had nothing to hide.

I am a French war correspondent assigned to cover the war in Vietnam, to report back and have articles printed from the North Vietnam viewpoint, to report short stories of their troops. I am doing a job I was sent here to do for my newspaper back in France.

The flight to Hanoi seemed short. I woke up a few hours before landing at the airport. It was early morning. The captain finally announced to the stewardess to prepare for landing.

"Here comes Jean Claude," I said to myself.

The plane began its final landing, and the wheels came down to lock into position before touching down. The plane touched the runway at higher speeds than normal and reversed the jet engines to slow down. The plane vibration was strong, with the doors of the overhead bins coming open and carry-on luggage falling. The runway was rough, and the plane bounced along as we taxied to the disembarking location.

When we finally reached the area to get off the aircraft, everyone scrambled to get off first. I waited to have more room to gather my backpack and walk off the plane. As I climbed down the airplane stairs, I noticed in the distance my welcoming policemen. I could feel their eyes on me, waiting for my arrival. I went toward them with the attitude of wellness to get my entry into North Vietnam over with and get on with my mission. They turned and let me pass into the terminal.

I came into the airport terminal, and everyone stared at me, likely wondering who I was and what I was doing in their country. Just as I walked through the terminal door, soldiers escorted me to a small room and the interrogation began. At first, I was skeptical, nervous I might slip up and speak in English. But I stayed focused; I kept my eyes aimed at the person asking questions.

Inside, however, my life flashed in front of me. I didn't want to be killed in this hellhole. I kept telling myself, "Jean Claude, stay cool and focus on your mission; just be yourself. Remember, these people are doing their job, it's a process of making sure you are who you say you are."

Maybe I should have taken that cook job, go home in ten to twelve months, see Sofie and all my friends, and continue skiing. That would have been easier. Yet here I was, deep behind the enemy line, seeking to find out all I could about their war plans for the south.

I was interrogated by a higher-level airport security officer who asked me every kind of question imaginable. This first encounter with the North Vietnamese security police lasted about thirty minutes. They took my identification cards and camera equipment and told me they would return them to the French Embassy within three days. I was told to stay at the French Embassy housing facility until I was approved by the authorities.

Two escorts put me into a Russian jeep and drove me to the embassy's front entrance, where security police explained to the Vietnamese guards that I wasn't to leave the compound until I had the war correspondent identification seal stamped into my passport and laminated photo identification press card. Once I had these two very important IDs, I was allowed to leave. Surprisingly I received these identifications quickly the next morning.

After receiving the official identification, I was off to the Vietnam News Bureau to make arrangements to see Dien Bien Phu. I was received by escorts assigned to me by the News Bureau of North Vietnam. They came by the French Embassy at 06:00 to pick me up in the morning. The escorts, Ms. Hue and Mr. Dang, were friendly and made me feel important. They had an interest in knowing more about me and what I would like to see and write about while they were my escorts. Ms. Hue, wanted to know about France because she wanted to go there and study at a small college.

So far, everything was falling into place. The trip to Dien Bien Phu was dusty and seemed like a long way. We stopped at a military depot for gasoline for our jeep, where I offered the escorts lunch, and they accepted. We all agreed to have a short lunch break and bring along drinks and food to have at Dien Bien Phu.

We arrived late in the afternoon just before it got dark. I took a few photos, but we had to stay overnight in military barracks. The next morning, we met at 07:00 to have breakfast and make plans for the day. They took me to the most important places in the battle for pictures, and I asked them questions. I must say it was interesting to see and hear the details of this engagement. I wanted to get all the details so I could write a different news article on Dien Bien Phu.

My escorts had a few insights that were different. I wanted to capitalize on their knowledge of the battle, and I told them I would give them a byline for helping me. They were pleased to know I would include them. I would probably have these two escorts with me full-time while on this assignment. So, my goal was to make them feel comfortable, have trust in me, and I let them know I wanted to write stories about the war from their viewpoint. I would see if this strategy worked.

Before dropping me off at the embassy, I told them, "I will have the news article finished tomorrow morning. I want you to read it and see if you have anything to add."

We then headed way back to Hanoi, where we got in late at night. Ms. Hue and Mr. Dang took me to the French Embassy. I had brought back gifts from France that could be used for trust-building, just in case I needed to impress someone. When I gave them each a gift, they were surprised and had smiles on their faces.

I was tired from the trip and needed a long shower. I would see if I could get into the kitchen to get a snack before going upstairs to my room.

CHAPTER 12
THE BANQUET

The next morning after returning from Dien Bien Phu with my two escorts, I received a message from the News Bureau office in Hanoi, inviting me to attend a formal dinner party with the Vietnam military command and other diplomats from Russia, Cambodia, and Laos. All these officials would have their spouses, staff aides, and members of their families.

It would be a swamp full of information for me to gather. It was a must for me to reach my handler and asset in Hanoi. I would need a spy camera wristwatch to take photos of all the right people attending the occasion. But how would I get away from the two spies I have glued to me all the time?

Finally, I had a break from them. I dressed in disguise and ventured out in the evening. I walked near the French embassy, hoping to reach a contact. As instructed, I left identifiable chalk marks on the electric pole with an unusual iron bench near the east side of the French Embassy.

I kept thinking about how I only had two days to get ready for this event. I needed to get a suit, a white shirt, a tie, and dress shoes. I didn't think they would appreciate my smelly old combat appeal. I would have to go shopping around Hanoi. It was difficult to find the right size. I shopped with my two escorts for one whole day and finally found a shop that would tailor-make a suit for me and they also had white shirts. I had all my items for the event and will be ready for my first debut. All I needed now was my contact to bring me the special equipment I requested.

In my sleep, I was hoping all night that my suit would be ready the next day as promised. My asset would have what I asked for to gather all the information that would be needed for the party. Wouldn't you know—my first assignment, all the VIPs from Southeast Asia in one room? I could end the war with one bomb.

My strategy was to meet as many high-ranking generals as possible as well as the general's aid staff and politically connected couples, and arrange photo interviews. We would see how well I made out with this assignment.

Unfortunately, getting into the ballroom wasn't a snap. The security was extremely high, and I felt that all the eyes in the room were watching me. I was young and handsome, with brown hair and blue eyes.

They must have been saying to themselves, "What is this man doing here? I must find out who he is and why is he here."

I moved around very slowly and cautiously. The room was full of brass, and I could feel the tension choking me. I was surrounded by seasoned spies on my first assignment. Other war correspondents were attending the banquet. They were seasoned and had been there before and had a history with the establishment. It was a real break for me. I had to be cool, and I couldn't tell too many stories about France. However, the newspaper in France recommended me very highly to the News Bureau here in Hanoi. I would use this résumé to my advantage to capitalize on moving to the top leaders of North Vietnam, Russia, Cambodia, and Laos.

I came across one couple, the French ambassador Jean Burnet and Mrs. Therese Burnet. We exchanged light conversation and once he knew it was safe, the ambassador motioned with his head for me to follow. We excused ourselves and went into the restroom. Because he couldn't give me the package in the open, he had used a cloth towel and placed the wristwatch inside. Then he placed the towel in a small basket near the exit door. I followed him and picked up the towel with the camera inside and placed the watch on my wrist. All CCTV cameras in the restroom were blocked by my position in the restroom from seeing any suspicious actions.

I continued to visit with the French Ambassador and his wife throughout the night. I wanted to share with them the optics of being attentive. I also wanted to let the other people in the ballroom know I was with my ambassador.

It was a highly emotional evening for me. I couldn't fall on my face; once again, I had to be cool. I found myself dancing with beautiful, attractive ladies. The room was full of gorgeous daughters from their countries. I could feel by their body movements and conversations they were scouting for love. I moved my hand up and down their backs.

"I heard that Frenchmen are enjoyable, and exciting in bed," The lady from Laos whispered in my ear in French.

I looked her in her eyes and commented, "I haven't heard anything like that, but maybe it's true."

In this room were the most attractive ladies from North Vietnam, Russia, Cambodia, and Laos. This was exciting for me. Like a fox in a chicken house, I could move around the room with these ladies and try to charm them. They crawled all over me when I told them I was from the French Alps area and lived in Thonon-les-Bains. I told them I was a war correspondent working for a newspaper in France. This conversation was exciting to most of my new ladies' friends.

Now I had to find the most valuable ladies of the night. If I could have three or four ladies who could give me cover for my missions, and I could find safe houses in their country, this would be ideal. I became interested in the lady from Laos. She was very friendly toward me. I went after her like a great white shark. We danced together several times. I was impressed by her ability to speak French.

This would be great—yes, they couldn't go into the combat area but being seen here with them in front of these generals and their aides would be beneficial. This connection with them and their parents would open doors I wouldn't have otherwise. What a gift. The timing was perfect for me. It would open doors for me to move in and get the stories I was looking for. This party was my threshold to getting into the know.

While dancing with my lady from Laos, I noticed a Russian officer dressed in full uniform. He looked interesting. He was young, strong, physically fit, had blonde hair, and was very serious. Covered with medals and other rewards, he reminded me of the red-tail hawk overlooking possible prey. I wanted to approach him and introduce myself. However, I was very dubious and skeptical. I hoped I could have a chance to meet him, maybe an introduction to another high-ranking Russian officer. That would be the best way.

He was a reserved, quiet, in-the-background, low-key individual. The kind of personality you might want to stay away from. However, he intrigued me. I wanted to get to know him; how could I innocently meet him? I couldn't bring suspicion into my introduction. This Russian officer was handsome and young, and maybe one of my lady friends of the evening could break the ice. It would be better if they approached him. He would accept the offer to dance or he could refuse. How could he refuse any of these princesses in front of his superiors? He must dance with her.

He accepted the reaching hand of the Cambodian lady—only a self-righteous fool would refuse her hand. She had an exciting, happy personality and was very attractive. The trap was set. I moved with my dancing partner closer and closer to him, and now I was close to the lady from Cambodia.

"*Voudriez-vous nous rejoindre à notre table?*" I said to him. (*Would you like to join us at our table?*)

"*Vous êtes Français?*" he asked me. (*You are French?*)

"*Mais bien sûr,*" I replied. (*But of course.*)

I continued our conversation in French. "From your nameplate, I see your name is Gorky. My name is Jean Claude Martin. I represent the French newspaper *La Combat-Haute-Savoie.* I am a war correspondent taking photos and writing stories about the Vietnam War seen from the North Vietnamese viewpoint. The readers are interested in getting stories about this conflict. I would like to have the opportunity to be placed near the North Vietnamese and Viet Cong camps along the western borders of Vietnam and possibly report on their skills and military conflicts. I would also enjoy having an interview with you at your convenience, Mr. Gorky. How can I stay in contact with you?"

Gorky gave his information card to me.

"I apologize for not addressing you as Colonel Gorky," I replied in French. "I am not familiar with the Russian military chain of command."

I didn't want to give him the idea that I might know the difference. You might call this playing naive. After all, I am a French reporter.

"Jean Claude Martin . . ." Colonel Gorky said in French, "I checked your background thoroughly this morning before our engagement this evening. The airport security police brought your file to the Russian Embassy the morning after your arrival. My staff has passed your clearance and I feel comfortable giving you a limited interview. If I feel this interview is worthwhile, I will divide other interviews into segments. When I have more experience with your reporting and printed news articles, you can have another interview. Maybe you can get me promoted to general."

"Only if you help me become the top war correspondent," I said.

69

"Let's meet tomorrow morning at the Russian Embassy at ten a.m.," Colonel Gorky said. "My aid will come and get you into the building. After the interview, I will need to read your article before you send it to France. No photos will be taken of me—*ever*. Are these conditions acceptable to you?"

"Yes," I replied, "but I would like to have more than a whitewash interview. I am looking for a meaty interview with teeth."

"I don't know if I can give you that," Colonel Gorky said. "I will answer your questions; however, if there are questions I can't answer, I will explain to you why. Off the record, of course. Excuse me, Jean Claude, I must have the last dance from the Lady of Cambodia before I excuse myself from this delightful evening. I'll see you tomorrow morning. Don't be late."

He shook my hand and asked the lady for a dance. The colonel appeared to be relaxed and enjoying himself with his partner as they spun around the dance floor. The first volley of our conversation was very informative.

I couldn't wait for tomorrow's interview. I was up most of the night writing and organizing my questions, getting the right wording.

CHAPTER 13
THE INTERVIEW

I arrived at the Russian Embassy on time and was escorted to Colonel Gorky's office. I quietly viewed his office, which was loaded with memorabilia, and made mental memories of everything. I could see hidden cameras and voice-recording equipment. Maybe people were watching me. I acted inquisitive but not nosey.

Shortly, Colonel Gorky entered his office.

"How are you today after last night's festivities?" Colonel Gorky asked in French.

"I had a grand time meeting all the people attending the event," I said. "I met unique, intriguing, and engaging people. The food was out of this world and the young princesses of the night were eager to meet us. I looked around the ballroom and you and I were the youngest there. With the most beautiful ladies at the banquet."

"Are you set up for the interview?" Colonel Gorky asked.

"I am, Colonel Gorky," I replied.

The colonel began his story. "My name is Dima Gorky. I am a special forces commander from the Russian military intelligence agency, a branch of the well-known KGB committee for state security."

I was flabbergasted.

Colonel Gorky continued. "I am trained in the fields of advanced martial arts, small arms, and personnel management. I came to North Vietnam as a lieutenant colonel and was selected from a large field of other candidates to go to North Vietnam to train elite soldiers in January 1964. I am fluent in other languages—French, Finnish, and I learned Vietnamese before going to North Vietnam. I spent over a year training in North Vietnam. Generals from the North Vietnamese command staff wanted me to go into South Vietnam and repeat the training tactics with the Viet Cong. This mission was very challenging and took more time to organize the teams. The idea of training the Viet Cong in South Vietnam was too dangerous, and I presented a plan to train in the bordering countries of Laos and Cambodia. The commanding generals in North Vietnam agreed and supported my plan."

Colonel Gorky paused, then said, "This ends our first interview. I have been to France but not to Haute-Savoie."

"I would enjoy showing you the French Alps one day," I replied. "It's a breath of fresh air, crisp and cool. You can smell the mountains. There are small restaurants that have extraordinary meals, and attractive ladies, of course. Once again, Colonel Gorky, if you can find the time while you are here, let me know what arrangements can be made, and we'll go to France. When will I see you again? Where do I leave my news article? How can I contact you?"

"So many questions," Colonel Gorky replied. "To start with: Leave your news article tomorrow morning at the Russian Embassy entrance. Address it to me, and I will read it shortly afterward. You can contact me through the front entrance. I will contact you by reaching out to the French ambassador. I must tell you that I am very busy with my work. I don't want to give you the wrong impression of me."

"Being in your position you must have a lot of responsibilities," I said. "Sir, without further ado, I will leave you to your work."

"I will read your article and make any changes," Colonel Gorky said.

"It will be at the front gate for you to pick up. Once you have made the changes, bring me the article back and leave it at the front gate again."

"Can someone at the Russian Embassy deliver a package to the French Embassy for me to pick up? I will make any changes and return the article for your approval," I replied.

"Yes," Colonel Gorky replied.

I left his office and headed back to the French Embassy, laughing all the way. Maybe I had dreamt up my interview with Colonel Gorky. This interview would be a big event in the news media. What an event for me as a freshman correspondent—having an interview with this high-level KGB Russian officer!

The next afternoon, I picked up the envelope at the front entrance of the Russian Embassy. Colonel Gorky left me a note, which said, "We will have another interview in the future. I will contact the French Embassy."

If Lieutenant Colonel Miller could see me now, his teeth would fall out of his head. He probably wouldn't believe me.

When I returned to the French Embassy, I had a message from my asset, which read, "What am I doing? I was in over my head and pulled back." I left a message for the asset to meet me for a face-to-face conversation inside the French Embassy quarters.

At this meeting, I said in French, "Friendly contact was made and I am inside the war room with Colonel Gorky."

They wanted to know about Colonel Gorky because they had never heard of him before.

"I just finished an interview with him," I explained.

They wanted to read the interview immediately. I also told them that Colonel Gorky gave me strict conditions for our interview, and I gave him my word. I went on to explain that I would have future interviews with Colonel Gorky, which would be in segments. I explained to my asset that Colonel Gorky wanted more experience with me and to get to know me. I also mentioned that I volunteered to take him to the French Alps.

My senior handler in Hanoi, Mr. Hong, was very much into himself. He gave me the impression that he was on top of all operations going on in Hanoi. He wore western suits in colors of tan, cream, and brown with a cream-colored Panama straw hat. His shoes were of poor taste and they didn't match his dress style.

"What!" Mr. Hong exclaimed in French.

"I have nothing to hide in France; I am clean," I replied. "I must build trust with him and become close to him to learn about his mission in Vietnam, so I can report back to Nha Trang about what is going on with the military strategy in Vietnam, Laos, and Cambodia. I think Colonel Gorky is more than a colonel in the Russian military advisory team in North Vietnam; he is also colonel in the KGB. His mission is very important here, and I am getting his trust. I have started to win his confidence. I am asking that you let me find out all I can about this Russian spy. Let me dig into his history and what he is doing here. You stated that you did not know Colonel Gorky. I will introduce him to you through my articles. I am looking forward to more interviews and going into the field with him. Sir, it is a win-win situation."

After some time thinking about my situation, Mr. Hong reluctantly agreed to let me press forward with Colonel Gorky. I agreed that I would do one or two more interviews with the colonel and maybe go into the field with him. I was happy to have the chance to explore some of the work that Colonel Gorky had done with the war effort.

CHAPTER 14
HO CHI MINH TRAIL

In Hanoi, Mr. Hong gave me the assignment to go along the western border of North Vietnam and into Laos with a small NVA patrol company. I had two days to get ready.

"You will meet up with Major Tuan Vu," Mr. Hong stated. "He is expecting you to join his company of NVA soldiers. You must go to the military post just west of the train station. You can take a cyclo to the front gate of that military compound.

"Give the guards this letter. You will be traveling in a truck convoy to Laos's encampments. Once you reach the first camp, you will head south the following day on the so-called 'Ho Chi Minh trails to the southern locations of Laos. You will follow Major Vu's lead. Get all the hometown news releases you can. Get stories of his soldiers. Major Vu will read your articles and decide to

Bamboo bridge in Laos near the Ho Chi Minh trail.

send them back to Hanoi for publication in the local newspapers. You will be going on short patrols with Major Vu or one of his assigned lieutenants. Go with them and absorb all the information you can. Make sure you get photos of Major Vu and his officers, and make them feel important. Ask for an interview. This would be beneficial for us to have on record. Also, you will need to take photos of anything worth recording for the G-2 Section in Nha Trang. Here are two special cameras, almost impossible to detect. Your assets will meet you along the way. Give them all the intelligence information you have."

Mr. Hong continued my instructions. "You must use the following hidden locations for the exchange with your assets: One location is, to put down the bicycle seat support pole and tie a small piece of cloth around the bicycle seat post. Another exchange location is inside the front bicycle tire. You will lace a cloth around the bicycle tire. You can also attach the information underneath an iron park bench's back leg on the left side. Finally, you can use the inside of an empty water bottle and place it by the left back leg of the bench. If you cannot see these drop-off locations, keep looking on your way south. Your assets will be looking for you in large villages along the way. If you do not have a chance to drop off your intel, I will meet you in Salavan. I have a safe house there and once I see you and make eye contact, follow me to an iron bench in front of the house. Most likely, there will be children playing in the street. Just sit down on that bench and watch the children play. You will then place your information as explained to you already.

"If you get into combat, pick up a dropped rifle to defend yourself," Mr. Hong stated. "You might see US or South Korean special forces—don't shoot. However, if you see drug-running gangs or smugglers, shoot to kill. Make your actions look real. You will be watched by the NVA officers and any escorts you might have on this trip. Remember, this convoy is supplying the Viet Cong in the south. The drug gangs and smugglers want these supplies to equip themselves or sell the items for money. You will have different talented personnel on this trip too. All of them will likely wonder what you are doing and won't trust you. They want to kill you! Don't give them an excuse to execute you. Be careful of the American forces in Dang Ha Mountain. Good luck and be careful!"

Places along the Ho Chi Minh trail, somewhere in Laos.

Jean Claude Martin's spy camera used to capture many of these photos.

Two of the roads on the Ho Chi Minh trail.

Treehouses on our journey down the Ho Chi Minh trail. Safe from large snakes and tigers.

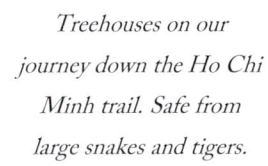

Overnight lodging and outdoor bath facility near Nong, Laos.

Viet Cong commander's "ghost house" outside of Nong, Laos.

*Road dividing Cambodia (left) and South Vietnam (right).
It was also used at night to move troops into South Vietnam.*

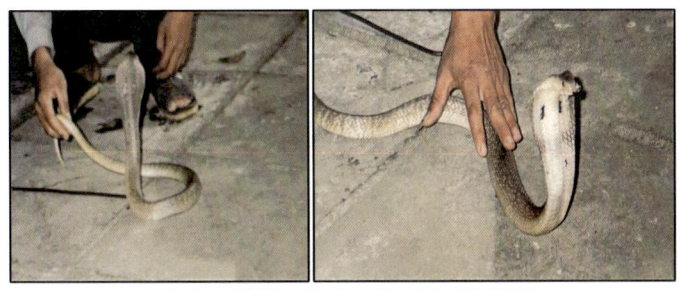

"Lunchtime" on the Ho Chi Minh trail in Southern Laos.
Had boiled snake meat with vegetables, fruit from the trees nearby,
rice, and raw honey from a hive hanging from a tree close by.

Three Viet Cong homes in Cambodia near Tây Ninh.

The convoy left Hanoi and traveled on the first day to Nhien Pu Luong, North Vietnam.

On the second day, we traveled to Vieng Xay, Laos. Here, I saw what the handler was talking about when he mentioned smugglers with drugs going into China. They didn't give us any trouble, just looked. I had a chance to take photos of them.

We came to Phonsavan and rested there for one day and night. I took many secret photos of this area. It is known as the Plain of Jars. I saw one of my assets at a market the next morning and managed to give him all the film and notes gathered so far. This leg of our trip would be the longest as we traveled day and night to get to Vieng Thong, Laos.

Midway through this section of the trip, we met a group of supporters. They were Montagnard (French for "mountain people"). It was exciting for me to see that this Montagnard village was full of spirit. Major Vu was taken aback by the reception. This was the first time I saw him relaxed on this trip.

I took several rolls of photos of him and these villagers and wrote stories about our stay with these Montagnard people. I gave Major Vu all the materials about our visit. Montagnard villagers went ahead and prepared a warm meal for us. The ingredients for this meal I have never seen nor eaten before—brown snake, monkey meat along with their warm brains, goats on a slow-moving spitter, chickens, vegetables, and a large quantity of rice.

The complete convoy personnel and I sat around two monster fire pits. The food was tasty and my appetite went toward the chicken, vegetables, and rice. The drinks were coconut milk, some type of sake, and water. I had coconut milk and water. At the end of this feast, the Montagnards gave us a musical performance. The female villagers danced and sang to their music with primitive bamboo instruments.

I had the freedom to walk around the village the next morning and take some more photos as well as write notes on what had happened and look for any valuable military intel. In general, the Montagnard villagers were friendly, and the younger population was eager to speak in French. I had a good time with these mountain people.

Montagnard crossbow

Montagnard morning market near Pleiku and Laos.

After we had breakfast, we were on our way down the Ho Chi Minh trail once again. We traveled through major supply routes, going toward

Nang Khang (known as "bomb village"), to Nape Pass, Mu Gia Pass, and Ban Karai Pass. I could stay here for days studying the passes and the value they have for the success of supplying to the south. It would be very interesting to see the interworking of the North Vietnam military strategy at this location. Boy, I have had fun recording all this information and mapping out the locations for the intel in Nha Trang.

We arrived the next morning after driving all night. I was tired from the long rough ride, but I could see firsthand the massive depots of suppliers headed to the south. I had the thought that one bomb could be very damaging and put a halt to the supplies. I needed to rush my report to my assets about the map coordinates with other important intel on these passes, such as how they are camouflaged from air surveillance. It is unbelievable how the Viet Cong covers these passes through this rugged terrain with available vegetation.

I was given an itinerary for the next few days; we would be going to Xepon, Nong, Ta Oi, Kaleum, Salavan, Sekong, and Attapu. At Attapu, we would be traveling on route 132 to Phouvong. This would then take us to Nhang, a major supply road into Pleiku. It could be dangerous, with drug-trafficking activity going on all the time. The military has engaged with drug gangs in this area in the past. Some of our troops have been killed and wounded. It was a hotbed for this type of business due to the drug route—there wasn't anything in this area for miles and nobody lived in this area but mercenary drug gangs and smugglers. The road into South Vietnam was passable and easy for the drug gangs to do business in South Vietnam with the American forces, Russians, and other distributors who supplied the general population with drugs.

We stopped in Salavan, Laos, for a break from riding the long distance, I walked around Salavan looking for the drop-off location when I saw Mr.

Hong on his bicycle. I followed him to his house and sat down on the iron bench in front and watched the children in the street. I relaxed, ate an apple, and drank water from a plastic bottle. After I finished the bottle of water and made sure all the water was out, I placed my rucksack in my lap covering the water bottle and any actions of putting all my intel inside the bottle. I then placed the bottle on the left back leg of the bench. Everything went as planned as Mr. Hong said it would, and I returned to the convoy ready to continue to Pak Nhai.

Major Tran ordered his officers and troops to gather around him for a silent prayer concerning Major Vu's passing back in the Nhang battle. Major Tran expressed his condolences to everyone. "Major Vu died a hero that day," Major Tran said. Major Vu will be missed for his efforts in the unification process in North and South Vietnam.

CHAPTER 15
ROAD TO PAK NHAI

We left for Pak Nhai, Ratanakiri, a province of Cambodia bordering Vietnam to the north and east. All of us were rested for the last leg of our journey.

The road was in good condition, and we would arrive at the compound by night. The small villages along the way were friendly and invited us to stop. Major Tran didn't want to stop, so we pushed forward.

East of Andoung Meas, near a Montagnard village, the lead truck got hit with an RPG, blowing the truck into the jungle and killing all the NVA soldiers on the truck. My jeep swerved to the left and went into the ditch. This time, I was carrying my AK-47 with several full magazines. I left my camera equipment in the jeep's back seat and went into action, shooting at the mercenaries that were coming toward us with rapid small-arms firing.

Soldiers from three other convey trucks became engaged in the fight. Mercenaries were coming at us from all angles. Bullets were flying all around me. Men on both sides were screaming and crying out.

I was using the jeep for cover—on the sides, underneath, keeping my backside blocked to avoid getting stabbed with a bayonet or shot.

RPGs were coming in, killing our soldiers and killing the mercenaries too. I continued to hold onto my area of the battle. This massacre lasted for about thirty minutes. Things slowed down to just five out of twenty NVA soldiers and four of the mercenaries.

Major Tran and Lieutenant Minh weren't hurt seriously, they suffered knife wounds in the legs, arms, and shoulders. I was hit in my right thigh—a clean muscle shot with a small-caliber pistol after stabbing a mercenary in the chest and neck. Lieutenant Minh came rushing to give me aid. He stopped the blood by putting pressure on the bullet hole. Lieutenant Minh continued to give me first aid and placed an NVA soldier to watch over me. I still had my AK-47 and ammunition to fight back if we were attacked again.

Our convoy was destroyed; we lost most of our supplies, ammo, uniforms, cooking utensils, all our medicine, and food. It took us several hours to get organized.

Major Tran was outraged about this incident. Once we got to the Pak Nhai compound, all of us were relieved. Major Tran ordered special patrols to look for mercenaries hiding in the jungle who took the lives of NVA soldiers. There were rumors that the CIA might have had a hand in these attacks, but there was no evidence to support this.

Major Tran and Lieutenant Minh got the others to load our dead NVA soldiers in the single truck that wasn't hit by an RPG. Then they finished giving first aid to others and moved what supplies we had into the other vehicles. Any vehicles that were beyond repair were destroyed.

We finally got loaded up and headed to Pak Nhai again. I was in the truck bed, lying on top of the supply boxes. Boy, this was a ride to remember. The road was rough and trees had fallen into the road. I had my fingers crossed that we would make it to the compound safely due to the rough road. With my position in the back of the truck, my wound began to bleed again. I tightened the bandage to put more pressure on the wound to stop the bleeding.

"Lieutenant Minh, how much farther do we have to go before getting to the compound?" I spoke up in French.

"I think by nightfall or around mealtime. I am not sure," Lieutenant Minh responded.

"Lieutenant Minh, would you mind keeping me informed?" I asked. "My wound has been bleeding but I tightened the bandage. I require medical attention once we get to the compound."

It was a long journey to the compound. The road was full of holes, causing us to stop and go all the time is aggravating. *God, please get us there soon. I need to get out of this truck and into a medical clinic.*

Finally, Lieutenant Minh told me, "Jean Claude, Major Tran has told me that the compound is nearby. I will have you taken to the clinic on the way into the compound to see our doctor there. You should be good as new within a few days."

"Thanks, Lieutenant Minh, for your help," I replied. "I appreciate it."

In a short period, which seemed like forever, we arrived at the compound.

CHAPTER 16
RECOVERY

Lieutenant Minh helped me into the medical clinic where a nurse came and laid me down on a narrow table and cut my fatigue pants off. She put iodine all over my leg and got it into my wound. I howled out from the sting, and the burning sensation was harsh. She washed my thigh and got the bullet holes ready for the doctor to put a few stitches in the front and back of my leg. There wasn't any medicine for numbing the bullet hole area; I just accepted the pain.

Enjoyable and peaceful places I saw in Laos.

More delightful places to relax peacefully in Laos.

Col. Dima Gorky returning from combat mission.

After the doctor finished sewing, another nurse came and gave me a body bath. Once I was cleaned and had clean clothes to wear, the nurse let me use some crutches to get around.

I needed something to eat. I asked the nurse if I could have something to eat and drink. She went away and came back with some food. I thanked her for the care she gave me. I ate and relaxed in the sun for a while. The sun felt good on my body, giving me a chance to recuperate from my ordeal. I started to doze off, and unknowingly, Colonel Gorky came to see me.

"Jean Claude, can I do anything to help you be more comfortable?" Colonel Gorky asked.

"Colonel, where did you come from?" I replied.

"This is my headquarters in Cambodia," Colonel Gorky said. "You're at the medical clinic inside the compound."

"How did you know I was coming?" I asked.

"I knew you were coming here days ago," Colonel Gorky said. "I found out yesterday that you were wounded. What are you trying to do, fight the conflict all by yourself?

"No, just want to stay alive," I said.

"The nurse put you here to relax," Colonel Gorky stated. "I need some time with you. I miss our conversations and exchanges of ideas. Major Tran wants to put an end to these raids from these mercenaries. He will probably ask you to help him organize special patrols to locate their strongholds and kill them. Jean Claude, I think you should lead the patrols; they seem to find you. If they gave you more soldiers to fight them, you would be good at doing this duty. Your first two combat encounters were very heroic. The skills you used to overcome your enemy were brilliantly done. I noticed your file back in Hanoi—you have been assigned to other war-torn countries to report the conflict."

"Could you make me a ranking brigadier general?" I replied.

Colonel Gorky laughed. "Even having a bullet hole in your leg, you still have a sense of humor. That is a sign of a good soldier. I am having a small dinner tonight, and I would like to invite you. I will check with the doctor to see if you are up for some fun. Jean Claude, you are special. You are one hell of a fighter. I am going to report your combat actions to my commanders. They will appreciate what you have done for us. I'll leave you for now and see the doctor. I will be back with the news."

The colonel's comments melted me. I was protecting myself. Anyone in that situation would have done the same. I was lucky to be alive and able to move around. This wound would heal soon and I would walk, run, and be able to have a normal life. I started to fall asleep again when the colonel returned.

Colonel Gorky informed me of the news. "Jean Claude, Dr. Loi has given me some pills for you to take. You take one in the morning and one at night. Please take one now with this water I brought you. Early this afternoon, we'll come and get you for dinner. Gets some needed rest; you will need your strength tonight."

"I thank you and everyone very much for the care given to me today," I replied. "It is hard to find the words to express my emotional appreciation."

"Someone will come and get you before we sit down for dinner," Colonel Gorky said. "You rest in the shade."

"Thanks, Colonel. I will see you later."

I was woken by a nurse, Ms. Sing, pushing my shoulder and asking me to wake up. She had a wheelchair for me.

"Can I try the crutches you gave me earlier?" I asked in French.

"Let us see if you can get up by yourself without having any help," Ms. Sing replied.

"Good question, let's see. How am I doing with your test?"

"I think you can handle the crutches," Ms. Sing said, "but no running with them. You are a good patient."

After I returned from Colonel Gorky's dinner, I called for Ms. Sing to put a new dressing on my wound. She was helpful to me and wanted to know if I wanted a new dressing in the morning. I told her after I had breakfast with the colonel, I would have someone notify her.

CHAPTER 17
Colonel Gorky's Second Interview

Colonel Gorky began in French. "Jean Claude, I believe you will become a top journalist in Southeast Asia before I become a general. The encounters you had near Nhang and east of Andoung Meas were impressive. I didn't know you could turn into a killing machine."

"Sir, I was simply defending myself," I replied.

"No, Jean Claude, the things I have heard about your combat skills from NVA officers have made you a hero in their eyes. Your name has become a household topic among us. Even my special forces people are looking for you to join them on combat missions. I will put you in contact with them."

"Sir, anyone would have defended themselves," I said to Colonel Gorky. "My profession is photojournalism. I was lucky; the attackers could have one extra round in their rifle, and it would have been curtains for me. Physically, I was stronger and overcame these thugs. I never killed another human before. In these moments of life-threatening engagements, my mind went into a focused trance. I've never experienced adrenaline so strong, giving me unmeasurable strength."

"Let's sit down and have our second interview before you become too famous," Colonel Gorky said. "The newspaper might find a desk job somewhere and you will be gone from Laos and Cambodia."

"My place is here," I replied, reassuring him. "Meeting you in Hanoi at the banquet was a miracle. I want to write stories about you. I believe you have experienced many combat conflicts that are a lot more courageous than my little incident. I am very interested in writing about your achievements. You speak French, making me feel like I am back in the French Alps. You inspire me; I am eager to write about your adventures here in Southeast Asia. You have an interesting background and I enjoy listening to you. Give me a chance to write and explore your accomplishments. I will have my newspaper in France spread your hardships and how you overcome them. There is a lot of information in your head. If you want to become a general, I can write about the work you are doing here in Laos, Cambodia, and Vietnam. I have done some investigating about you, Colonel, with other NVA officers while coming down the trails. I met engineers that know you and they told me how inventive you are. This group of engineers told me you are responsible for all the developments along the border of South Vietnam, improving the Ho Chi Minh trail. They also told me about taking orders from you. That you are the hero sitting in this office—'the architectural genius.'"

"When will you be ready for your interview?" I asked. "Let me know so I can get some writing papers. My writing supplies are dirty, wet, and full of wrinkles. I shall find some writing paper in the village."

"We have boxes of lined writing paper," Colonel Gorky said. "Help yourself and take what you need. I will tell my staff that you have permission to take it as needed. Come to this office tomorrow at oh-eight hundred for the interview."

I spent the rest of the day looking for clothing that would fit me. Also, I wanted to replace my rucksack. This one was torn, the back side ripped. I wasn't successful in finding another rucksack. The clothes were a little small but would work until I had a chance to shop in a larger village.

The next day, I arrived at Colonel Gorky's office for the second interview as planned.

Colonel Gorky looked at me and laughed.

"What is so funny?" I asked in French.

"Where did you get those clothes?" Colonel Gorky asked through laughter.

"At the mall," I said jokingly.

Colonel Gorky replied, "After the interview, go with Lieutenant Anh to the supply sergeant and get two sets of clothing that fit you. Maybe combat is just around the corner; you must have clothing that fits. Also, I'll have Lieutenant Anh find you another rucksack."

Before I officially began the interview, I asked Colonel Gorky, "What about the beautiful lady from Cambodia that you met in Hanoi at the banquet?"

Colonel Gorky nodded. "You will meet her again soon. I am having a party at my villa. You must join us; it will be enjoyable. I would be pleased to have you there with us.

Used French rucksack

There will be staff officers attending the party that have shown interest in having you come along on their missions into South Vietnam. This will give you a chance to get acquainted and find out which commanding officer you feel confident being with on these missions."

"Great, and I appreciate this opportunity to join them and write about their missions," I replied. "Shall we start your interview?"

Colonel Gorky began with his mission in Southeast Asia. "At the beginning of March 1965, I went to Laos, to the border province of Attapu, in the village of Sepon. During the first gathering, I met with the Viet Cong leaders and laid out the recruiting plans for the training of small insurgent teams in South Vietnam and using guerrilla warfare against the South Vietnamese and American forces. I set up meetings with the Cambodian Viet Cong commanding leaders to discuss training camps along the western border of Vietnam in remote locations. My second meeting was in Cambodia in Ratanakiri Province, known as the Golden Triangle, at Ten Salavay. The third meeting was in Mondulkiri Province at Bu Dam village, the fourth meeting was in Kratie Province at Lak Ke village, and the fifth meeting was in Svay Rieng Province at Chip Hou village.

"I brought with me each province leader who had the most skills to carry out future missions. These meetings were the highest level of secrecy in the North Vietnamese military command and the Viet Cong structure in the south. The intelligence was gathered from the first major encounter—the battle of La Drang, South Vietnam, which lasted from November 14, 1965, to November 18, 1965. With large-scale helicopter support, strategic B-52 bombers, accurate artillery fire, napalm bombings, and close-range air support, La Drang was the blueprint for the Vietnam War. The high command in Hanoi realized that my approach was the best strategy—small elite forces cause havoc wherever they could and attacking the American forces in a conventional war at La Drang was a military failure."

Colonel Gorky continued. "For each location, the timetable was extensive with a lot of details that had to be worked out. One of the main problems was logistics: Ho Chi Minh trails, which started to operate at the beginning of 1959, needed to be improved. Work camps were set up to connect old trails, going from the panhandle of North Vietnam southward, leading into South Vietnam around Da Lat. During my tenure in the region, the Ho Chi Minh trails could accommodate heavy trucks to most provinces and supply several hundred thousand active NVA troops in South Vietnam. This improvement was crucial to the successful invasion of South Vietnam.

"The Viet Cong had locations in place during the French occupation. For example, inside South Vietnam, close to Saigon, there is a city called Củ Chi with a deep tunneling complex with easy access from the nearby river as well as other secret underwater entrances leading into this complex. Củ Chi tunnels had the following: a cafeteria, storage for weapons of all types, rifle ammunition production, a hospital, fuel-storage tanks, and housing for large troops for insurgency missions. Other provinces along the western border of South Vietnam had underground support facilities—hospitals, fuel supplies, weapons, and cafeterias for potential advantages to launching attacks against their enemy military forces in South Vietnam."

Colonel Gorky went on. "I had success with this strategy in the south and was promoted to colonel in April of 1966 for performance in Southeast Asia. I requested from the North Vietnam command that each province have a Russian ranking officer and an equal NVA officer stationed at each training headquarters in Laos and Cambodia. I requested from the Russian commanding headquarters that more Russian officers and regular troops be assigned for combat duty in Vietnam. In general, they asked for a build-up of Russian soldiers in the region. I had big plans for the lunar new year in January 1968."

Colonel Gorky paused. "Using the waterways in Laos, Cambodia, and Ho Chi Minh trail, the supply routes were operating at a successful pace. Suppliers were getting through to the training camps in the south, and having a positive buildup of NVA and Viet Cong troops in the training camps produced elite teams to go into South Vietnam and attack targeted American encampments close to the borders. One very effective strategy we utilized was to attack with small forces during the early morning hours with tremendous mortar fire and 122 mm rocket bombardments. These attacks lasted for a few minutes, just long enough to cause psychological fear and casualties.

"The idea of these attacks was 'hit and run,' inflicting high casualties on the enemy forces and few casualties on the NVA and Viet Cong guerillas. I was instrumental in setting up other strategies, like having small, short tunnels where the forces could hide and come out to wound an enemy soldier on patrol. This action would require two other enemy soldiers to carry the wounded soldier. These enemy soldiers would encounter booby traps in different configurations while on their patrols. This would cause more enemy casualties and make it easier to ambush later that day or night. I insisted on a high ratio of twelve to one—twelve NVA and Viet Cong to one enemy soldier. This would be a massacre formula and psychologically demoralize the enemy.

"Another war strategy I used was to bring the war into the living rooms of American families. So, every day or night, different strikes on American forces would happen in South Vietnam to be televised in America.

American sons were getting wounded and killed, by both sides, and their parents didn't understand why the Americans had engaged the military in a war so far away. The strategy was working for us. Protests started at American college campuses; television news companies throughout the landscape covered the war. I was surprised by how well this scheme had captured the attention of so many people around the world."

Booby traps, with animal or human feces, found on South Vietnam trails in the jungle.

Tunnel entryways and exits.

Colonel Gorky continued. "In my last interview with you, I didn't want to tell you this, but I couldn't understand why the US forces didn't block the Ho Chi Minh trail's supply arteries into South Vietnam. They continuously engaged in conventional combat tactics, like not shutting down the Ho Chi

Minh trail or blocking the seaport at Kampong Saom Sihanoukville with their navy ships. We could bring tunnel-making equipment used in Russia into Cambodia to dig trenches for tunnel complexes. The Americans and their allies never put together any military strategies to halt our improvements of the roadways. This is the biggest mistake of the American war effort so far. This neglect gave us time to build up and bring heavy-artillery guns, tanks, and troops into place for upcoming attacks in South Vietnam that will happen over Tết in Vietnam."

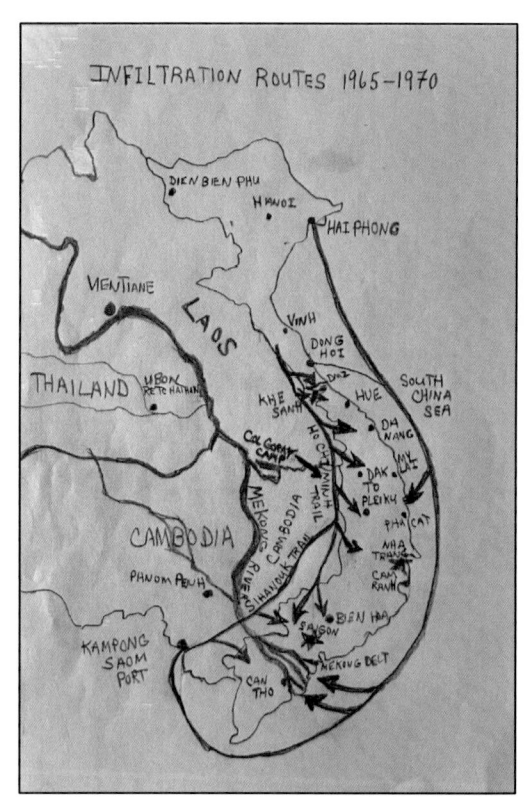

Colonel Gorky's camp, infiltration routes during the Vietnam War 1965–1970, and plans to supply the major cities in South Vietnam for the up-and-coming Tết Offensive in January 1968.

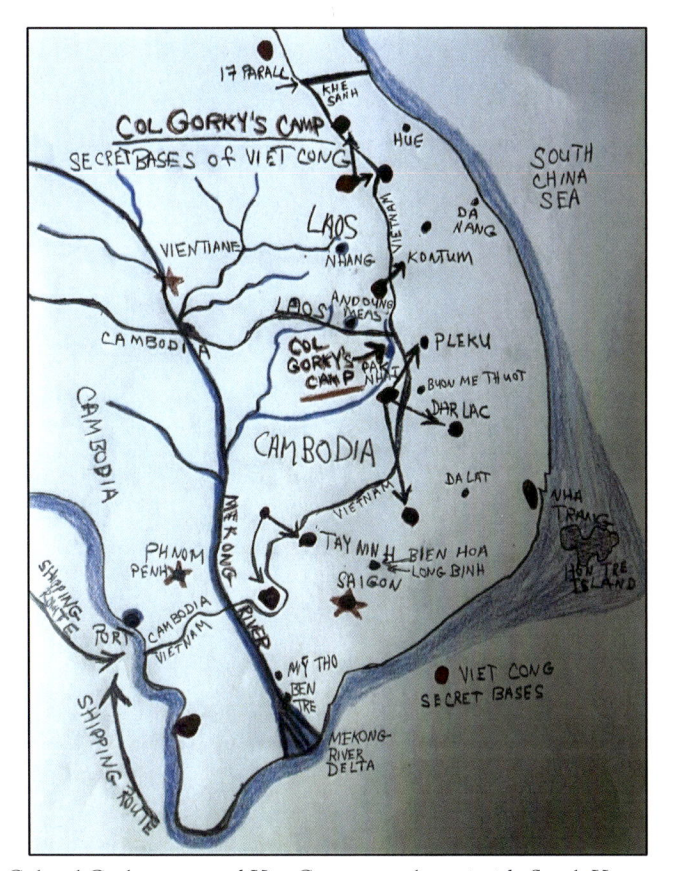

Colonel Gorky camp and Viet Cong secret bases inside South Vietnam.

Colonel Gorky continued. "I must add that if we are successful with the Tết Offensive, and the foreign military countries leave South Vietnam, these highway improvements will speed up our victory over South Vietnam. Our main objective in the Tết offensive will be Khe Sanh. This battle will be the Dien Bien Phu for American Forces. Do you know what happened to the French in Dien Bien Phu?"

"Yes, I do. The losses were great on both sides," I replied.

Colonel Gorky nodded. "I am confident that my military strategy will be successful. I have been planning this battle for several years." He paused. "Jean Claude, I have given you quite a story to publish. If you have any questions, please feel free to approach me or my staff. Once you get the interview ready for me to review, I want it hand-carried to me by you and we will read over the article together just in case there are corrections to be made. You must know by now that paid mercenaries want to kill me, for I interrupt their drug and smuggling operations. They would probably like to get their hands on you as well. We must be vigilant of our surroundings and be on guard during our stay here in Southeast Asia. I have troopers giving me security, but you, Jean Claude, have no one watching your back."

Colonel Gorky rose from his chair. "It's been a long day for both of us. Let us go and get something to eat before we retire for the day. You probably want tomorrow to write the interview. I am anxious to read your article. However, there were statements made by me that cannot be published. I was relaxed and told you too many secrets. I will line them out when I read your article."

"I will give you the complete interview with any changes you make for your approval," I replied.

"By the way," Colonel Gorky added, "you may want to add to your article that the Ho Chi Minh trail is mainly in Laos. The communists called it the 'Truong Son Strategic Supply Route.' The architectural engineer of the trail was Nguyen Cong Ho. He was responsible for the overall success of the trails turning into roadways."

"I will consider this very important information and weave it into our interview story," I concluded. "Let us go and get some food. I am famished."

CHAPTER 18
COLONEL GORKY'S SAFE HOUSE

Colonel Gorky's villa and compound near Pak Nhai, Cambodia.

As we walked into the kitchen, Colonel Gorky asked a Vietnamese man to cook us dinner. Our dinner consisted of chicken, local vegetables, sweet potatoes, and coconut milk with raw honey. Colonel Gorky didn't eat monkeys, snakes, or any other wild animal found in the jungle. I was glad and needed healthy food to eat. The village markets out here were not plentiful.

We enjoyed talking about good times, female relationships, and sports that each of us liked. I talked too much about my skiing experiences in France. I wanted Colonel Gorky to take me up on my earlier invitation about going to France with me. He didn't seem too interested in skiing, but maybe meeting a French lady or two was more appetizing.

After visiting and eating we went to our bedrooms. My room had a great view of the river. The veranda wrapped around the villa, giving a relaxing tropical surrounding. I started to write his interview article.

My impression of Colonel Gorky this evening changed. Maybe I was in over my head being around him. However, he appeared relaxed and open to my stories about my adventures. I kept telling myself that Colonel Gorky wasn't an angel, he was a colonel in the KGB. I needed to always watch myself and be careful about what I said and how I said it.

My God, I suddenly realized, *Colonel Gorky is the architect of the Vietnam War.* What if I was ordered to assassinate him? Could I do it? Would killing him stop the war in Vietnam? No one had the answers to these questions.

I needed to pass along all my intel about the Têt attacks on South Vietnam military encampments. I organized my intel for the handlers in Nha Trang, making sure I incorporated the details on how the Ho Chi Minh trail strategy was working for the NVA and Viet Cong.

Because my room was located directly next to Colonel Gorky's, I put a sheet over my head so no one would see my red light as I hastily wrote up my intel. I believed the room had hidden cameras inside the walls. Since I had all tomorrow to write Colonel Gorky's article, the pressure was on to finish collecting this information.

I finished my report for Nha Trang and filmed some of the documents on the secret camera to hand over to the handler. How could I meet them tomorrow? This was my chance to find out if the things I learned in France would work in the field.

The morning came and I started writing Colonel Gorky's article. His interview had been long and had a lot of information to sort out. In the afternoon before our next meal, I presented it to Colonel Gorky.

He took it and stated, "After our meal, I will read over the article and return it to you tomorrow morning to discuss any changes. This will give you time to rewrite it and get it ready for publishing."

CHAPTER 19
MAKING NEW FRIENDS

I couldn't believe my eyes as I walked into the dining area and looked across the room. There was Colonel Gorky's lady friend from the Hanoi Banquet. I was happy to see her and told her she was beautiful—the shining light of the evening. She received me with a kiss on my left cheek, and I returned a kiss on her right cheek.

"Where have you been hiding this lovely lady of the night?" I asked Colonel Gorky.

"She has a villa nearby," he replied.

"How convenient and romantic that must be," I said. "Can I put this arrangement in my article about how you are struggling with war planning in Southeast Asia?"

"Not with this article," Colonel Gorky replied, "but maybe in the future we can write another article about my lady of the night and have it published in France and Cambodia."

I looked at her and said, "She could be a model in France. I have a contact there who could open doors if she wanted to become one."

Both seemed to be interested in getting her into the modeling industry.

"I could be her manager," Colonel Gorky said.

"Yes, you could," I said, "and both of you could stay at my home in

Thonon-les-Bains. It would be easy to travel to Geneva where she would be working."

Colonel Gorky nodded. "Oh, by the way, we have a warm surprise for you."

"What is it?"

"Jean Claude, could you go into the kitchen and get us some French wine the maid has prepared? The wine is on the counter."

"Of course," I replied.

I went into the kitchen and there was my dancing partner from the Hanoi banquet. I couldn't believe what I was seeing. We embraced each other with a strong hug and kiss on each cheek.

With a loud voice, I called out to the other room. "Colonel Gorky, I think I am having a combat fatigue relapse. The lovely lady I danced with in Hanoi is standing in front of me."

In the dining room, everyone laughed.

I kissed the lady from Laos's cheek passionately again and again. She responded by kissing me on my lips. I was taken aback by her aggressiveness. I took her hand and we carried the wine to the dining area.

Colonel Gorky laughed. "How was that for an encore?"

"It has been an evening of surprises!" I replied. "First, your friend from Cambodia, having a gourmet meal, and now the lady from Laos. I don't have words to express my feelings, but I must tell you that I am extremely pleased to be here tonight."

"You need to know their names," Colonel Gorky said. "The lady from Laos is the daughter of Prince Vongkhamchanh. Her name is Angelina. And the lady from Cambodia is Princess Bopha Sovannar. Her father is the prime minister."

Colonel Gorky suggested we go out on the veranda after having dinner to enjoy the evening and talk about ourselves and what we might be doing tomorrow and the days ahead.

After a few moments of silence, I said, "Life is wonderful—I get to be with friends under the moonlight after having a tasty French dinner. This view of the river was breathtaking. So many people on Earth are dim and can't see the bright side of life. They cannot fathom exchanging their feelings with one another. Having the ability to express your feelings to loved ones and close friends is a gift. I want to know all I can about your countries. I like to learn about cultures and understand people. I see this as a learning experience and adventure, with people reaching outward for freedoms and fighting for their existence."

"Jean Claude, I didn't know you were a philosopher too," Colonel Gorky replied. "I must add to your statement about life: I agree, it is a gift and shouldn't be taken lightly. I remember many times my life flashed before me. I've experienced many combat engagements here in Southeast Asia—mercenaries wanting to kill me, government leaders having different opinions, and military officers looking for an avenue to get involved with the drug business, willing to kill for this chance. Villages in the Golden Triangle, and populated by the Hmong, Shan, Yao, and Lahu ethnic groups, control the drug trade. They use the waterways of Ruak and Mekong to move heroin. I have many problems with the drug business. Just between us, I have lower-ranking officers and troops who are involved in drug trading. A few of my officers and troops are hooked on the drug scene. We have set up a medical clinic for them and tried to help them break the grip heroin has on their bodies. I fear the decay in my forces here is serious. The Americans have a problem with this heroin dependency. Off the shore from Nha Trang, there is an island named Hon Tre where the Americans have a large hospital. At this facility, they treat this dependency, but I think it's worse here with my troops."

Suddenly, Colonel Gorky stopped before saying, "Let us talk about brighter topics than war stories."

We all agreed.

CHAPTER 20
NEW LOVER

"What do you enjoy doing? Where did you go to school and learn how to speak French?" I asked Angelina.

"I enjoy reading books and travel magazines, riding a bicycle, playing tennis, listening to music, and studying about different cultures, especially France," Angelina replied. "My mother is French, and she taught me the language. My father was educated in France and has citizenship in both Laos and France. My mother and father speak French most of the time when we are in our private living quarters of the palace. We've even traveled to Paris for the holidays a few times. As Colonel Gorky informed you earlier, my father is the prince of Laos. He is on the path to becoming the president of Laos."

Angelina continued. "A lot of my time is spent as the diplomat's daughter. I must tell you, my mother observed you back in Hanoi—your body language with me, how you danced with me, your facial expressions. She was curious about you and wanted to know why you were at that banquet. She contacted the French Embassy in Hanoi to find out more about you. Once my parents had more information about you and the report from Colonel Gorky, they gave me permission to come here and spend time with you."

Angelina's parents' villa near Colonel Gorky's compound.

Angelina went on. "I have been waiting here for days, but I knew you were coming soon from Colonel Gorky's reports. I want to get to know you and spend time, like tonight—talking about anything that comes to mind. Colonel Gorky has told me about your incident east of Nhang, and the village nearby—that you got shot in the thigh and had to have medical attention. I told my family, and we are very proud of your heroism. My father has asked me to invite you to our palace for a few days."

She then giggled and asked, "Can I see your scars of war?"

"I must get permission from Colonel Gorky to leave and travel with you," I replied. "I have obligations from my job in France; they expect news articles to flow into their office from me. I'll need a few days here before we go to your family's palace."

"Yes," Angelina said, "we can have tonight and the following days together here at Colonel Gorky's villa."

Moments later, the party joined us on the pathway to the river. As I was walking with the group, my mind wandered back to Sofie and how

I was going to handle this delicate situation. This role I had to play with Angelina was important to the overall mission of secrecy.

After the short walk to the river, we headed back to Colonel Gorky's villa to clean up from our party dinner.

Colonel Gorky pulled me aside and said, "Jean Claude, I have business with Angelina's father three days from now. I will be taking three of my staff officers with me. I don't know how long I will be at the palace in Vientiane, but I can bring you to the palace in my helicopter. You have said that learning about different cultures is high on your list of education. This is your chance to see a spectacular palace and a loving family. Angelina could escort you around the beautiful capital city. What a news story that could be back in France."

"Thank you, Colonel Gorky," I replied, then I turned to the ladies and said, "What has been said here tonight is like reading a fairy tale before going to sleep. It is powerful and overwhelming to think that I am in your company, sharing time in this villa with the presence of new friends. I come from a simple background—I was brought up with cows, horses, chickens, ducks, a large garden, and hunting."

"Colonel Gorky has told us a few things about you," Angelina said. "You have displayed kindness not only to Bopha and me but to Colonel Gorky and his staff. Jean Claude, it is delightful to be with you tonight. Can we go for a short walk around the villa compound?"

"I would love to," I responded then turned to Colonel Gorky and Bopha. "Thank you for a pleasant evening. Is it all right to walk in the villa gardens and go down to the river?"

"I will tell my guards and they will watch out for you," Colonel Gorky replied. "However, you may want to check in with Angelina's security staff before going anywhere."

"I appreciate your hospitality this evening and taking care of our beautiful ladies," I said. "What time shall we come for breakfast?"

"Breakfast is at 07:00 out on the veranda," Colonel Gorky said.

I nodded my head. "Have a good evening."

Riverboat on the Tonie San River near Colonel Gorky's property.

Dock and boathouse near Angelina's parent's private villa.

Angelina and I went for a stroll along the river's edge. As we walked out on the boardwalk holding hands, Angelina began to rub my hands in a very romantic gesture, as if she were asking to make love without saying a word. I had to put Sofie out of my mind during the passionate exchange of love. In my mind, I had to screen all my emotional feelings while I was with Angelina. Something like that would blow my cover and have me sent back to France—or worse, have me killed.

We came to the end of the pier and turned to face each other and exchanged passionate kisses. She started to move her hand down my leg. Once she touched my wound dressing, her kiss turned into a so-called "French kiss." I moved my hand to caress her beautiful body. She moaned for more touching and asked for us to rush to her villa.

We went past her security guards and directly into her bedroom. She slowly undressed, her body petite but athletic. She moved around the room, getting warm water and a washcloth to wash me. I removed my clothing, and was careful about my wound.

Both of us were intrigued by the other's bodies. She wanted to see my battle scars and bullet holes. As we softly touched and investigated each other, I felt the warmth of Angelina reaching out for my love. Her soft, sexy voice whispered in my ear how she had wanted me all night. According to her, I was the first man to make love to her. I grabbed a washcloth on the bathroom shelf to bathe her. I moved my hand slowly, touching her tenderly and gently with my strokes along her body. I gave her comfort and breathtaking love and stayed with her all night, into the early morning hours.

"Jean Claude, you mustn't leave—you have to stay with me!" Angelina whispered. "Don't go on these dangerous missions. What if something happens to you again? Right now, I don't believe I could find another like you."

"There will be more moments like this," I said softly, "and better emotional times as we begin to know each other better. As our relationship grows, our feelings will mature toward each other. But we should get dressed for breakfast with Bopha and the colonel."

Later, as we walked toward the villa for breakfast on the veranda, I told Angelina, "Last night and this morning will be memorable moments in our lives. I can't wait to make love to you again. I don't know what to expect from your family when I meet them, but I want them to understand that I am a gentleman with you. If your security team tells your parents about me staying the night with you, they need to hear my side."

"Jean Claude, I am a grown woman," Angelina replied. "My family trusts me and my judgment. Please don't worry."

When we approached the veranda, we spotted Colonel Gorky standing next to the railing.

Colonel Gorky smiled and said, "I see the night was very exciting and rewarding under the shining stars for the both of you. Did you have a good rest?"

At the same time, we answered, "Yes."

"And very romantically under the full moon," I added. "I have never seen the moon so bright and full of love."

"I have never heard a statement like that before," Colonel Gorky said. "I must write it down. Let us join Bopha at the veranda table and have breakfast."

Angelina and I greeted Bopha and took our seats at the table.

The maids served us a very delicious French breakfast with warm milk, croissants, brie, honey, and apples.

As everyone was busy eating breakfast, I thought that Colonel Gorky and Bopha must have had a great night together as well. The ladies had smiles on their faces—a good indication.

Finally, I broke the silence. "I would like to share my appreciation for a delightful evening with all of you and now this delicious French breakfast." I turned to Colonel Gorky and asked, "How did you find this place tucked away in the jungle?"

"I saw this property from the air by accident," he replied. "It was abandoned and rundown. I went to the local government authorities and asked about it, and they told me I could have it. I spent many years fixing this place, bringing materials in from different countries, having troopers make improvements to the gardens and buildings, and modernizing the plumbing throughout the villa. I enlarged this villa to what you see today."

"Did you have help with any of the designing?"

"No, I had ideas of what I wanted and how it should look," Colonel Gorky explained. "Coming from northern Russia and traveling in many European and Southeast Asian countries gave me the inspiration for most of the garden layouts and building designs. Some of the buildings were already here."

"This is a magnificent architectural achievement," I said. "To change the subject, do we have a meeting tomorrow morning about departing for the Presidential Palace?"

"Yes, later this morning—maybe over lunch—we will confirm our trip," Colonel Gorky replied.

CHAPTER 21
GOING TO THE PALACE

The Presidential Palace in Vientiane, Laos (photographer unknown).

"Have you decided on traveling with Angelina?" Colonel Gorky asked. "Your invitation to the Presidential Palace by the royal family is a big deal for you, Jean Claude."

"Maybe I will have a chance to get an interview with Angelina's parents," I replied. "It would be a wonderful experience." I continued, "I am planning on going to Vientiane with Angelina when she leaves."

"I'll call her father after breakfast and put Angelina on my phone to ask about your visit."

"I appreciate your generosity," I replied. "If her parents accept my trip to Vientiane, I would like to go to Pak Nhai, Cambodia, and purchase gifts for them—a token of respect and appreciation."

Colonel Gorky nodded. "We will see what her parents say. I will arrange a jeep to take you into town."

"Could Angelina come along with me to help with ideas on what to buy for her parents?" I asked.

"Jean Claude, you are making this arrangement more difficult. Once we get the green light from her father, I will have my staff find out about the transportation."

"Could I borrow a pistol, preferably a .32 with a silencer?" I asked. "I have experience with this setup in France and coming down the trails in Laos. I could help protect Angelina. I don't have any weapons with me."

"I will get you a weapon," Colonel Gorky replied, "but I don't know about the caliber. We have different calibers here. You will have some type of pistol going into town. You must return it to me once you get back. But, Jean Claude, you don't need a weapon! You are a ninja."

I laughed. "I don't digest lead bullets very well. I would feel better if I had a weapon with me, just in case anything happens in town. If Angelina gets hurt, it will be on my conscience forever."

Colonel Gorky nodded then said, "Please excuse me. I am going to call Angelina's father and put her on the phone. Angelina, if you would please follow me to my office to talk with your family."

Angelina rose from her chair, then said to me, "Jean Claude, come with us. You might have a chance to speak with my mother."

I smiled. "Thank you, I would like to join you."

On the phone call, they discussed Colonel Gorky's upcoming visit. Once they finished with the details, the conversation moved to my visit. Angelina received the phone and began talking with her father in French. They discussed her visit to Colonel Gorky's villa, how she was getting along with his staff. Her father asked about me and how long she would be staying at Colonel Gorky's villa. Angelina explained she wanted to invite me and return with Colonel Gorky. Her mother expressed her wishes for me to join them. Angelina finished talking with her parents and hung up the phone.

The colonel decided for us to travel to the Presidential Palace in Vientiane that morning. I went to my bedroom and changed my clothing so my handler would be able to identify me.

I was going to have a chance to see why Colonel Gorky was visiting Angelina's father. I would be able to see who was attending the meeting and why it was so secret for Colonel Gorky and his senior military strategist staff.

CHAPTER 22
THE HANDOVER

Events were coming together. I was going to hand over my intel to the handler, Mr. Cuong, in Pak Nhai. It would be tricky with all the security around us but I needed to get this intel back to Nha Trang. A lot was at stake for our troops in South Vietnam.

Security was arranged for Angelina. I had a Russian pistol without a silencer, but it was better than nothing. Three jeeps and a small three-quarter-ton truck, used to carry armed troops, were lined up in the courtyard. I had all my documents and film disguised with me. I was ready to board the second-in-line jeep.

Angelina came out of her villa dressed in native clothing. She looked beautiful in her colorful dress as she got into the jeep with me. And then off we went.

Angelina and I rode in the second jeep until we were halfway to Vientiane. The jeeps stopped and her head of security asked us to move to the third jeep and cover up with the blanket. This section of the road had a history of hijacking activities. The remainder of the ride into the village seemed short.

At the center of the village, we stopped and everyone carefully got out of the jeep. The security team surrounded Angelina as we walked into the open market area.

I was separated from them most of the time, giving me a chance to be recognized by my handler. I moved around to different visible locations, while still staying close to Angelina and looking for possible gifts for her parents. Hunting for gifts gave me the excuse to meet my handler in this village.

After shopping and looking for some gifts that would be different, we sat down to have some lunch as a group. The security team separated into different areas around the outdoor cafe.

During our meal, a young boy and girl came to our table asking for money and handed us a flier on renting bicycles. The rental shop was just around the corner. Angelina asked her security team leader if we could rent two bikes and ride around the village. I realized that this could be my handler's way of contacting me.

The security leader didn't want Angelina to go, so I asked if I could go and look, just out of curiosity. I also asked if Angelina could ride around the village with me if I got the bikes. After a moment of hesitation on his part, the security leader allowed me to go and check out the bike shop.

Finally, I had a chance to hand over the intel. Inside, my heart was jumping. I could hear it thumping. I was extremely relieved to have the chance to be alone for a few minutes. Just enough time to hand over my material. I needed to be discreet about my movements, just in case Colonel Gorky or someone else had spies watching me. I had all my intel in a colored water bottle. My plan was to pretend I finished the bottle of water and needed to throw it away.

As I got closer to the shop, a man repairing a bike gave me one of our secret codes. I knew right away he was my handler. He looked like a bicycle shop owner, with his baseball cap and small mustache, bent over and repairing a bicycle rim.

Mr. Cuong, a handler in Pak Nhai, Cambodia.

He had a small frame and an interesting face. I began casually talking with him and mentioned I was interested in renting two bikes. At the same time, I pretended to drink water. Once I got the information about the bike rentals, I acted as if I was finished with the water bottle and moved to throw it away. Instead, I put the bottle into a hidden pocket of the handler's jacket, which hung close to the ground behind him. From the road and each side of the shed, no one would be able to see where I put the empty bottle.

I moved away and shook his hand, then walked away. As I did, I turned slightly to see what my handler might be doing. Someone came out of the shop and replaced my handler as he disappeared. I didn't look back again as I met back up with Angelina and her group.

When Angelina saw me, she asked, "Can we rent bikes at the shop?"

"Yes," I replied, "and I have all the information for us to read before we decide where we want to go. I think they will let us rent the bikes at a very low price. Have you found any gifts for your parents?"

"I found three items that my mother would consider unusual," Angelina said. "They are primitive musical instruments. I would like to buy all three of them and hang them in my bedroom back home to remind me of you running around in the jungle with the Montagnard villagers."

I smiled as I responded. "I don't know about me running around in the jungle, but these musical instruments are very interesting to me. I like the idea of hanging them on your bedroom wall. I will help you when we get to your home. It will be fun, and I like decorating. Back home in France, my home has primitive furnishings. One day, I will take you there and show you. You will enjoy my home. It isn't a palace but close to it."

Angelina laughed. "Jean Claude, you are so funny. We can make it our palace. I want to see how you live—look around the countryside and visit with your family and friends."

"I don't know if I can let you visit my village," I said. "All my male friends will be chasing you and making me jealous. Maybe you will play with me and make them more determined to get into your underwear."

"You have a vivid imagination to think that I would play with our love," Angelina replied. "Let other men try to get into my underwear. I don't wear underwear, you know that."

"Angelina, you make me laugh. You are very delicious, cute, and funny."

Angelina changed the subject. "Will you describe your home in the Alps?"

"You can see Mont Blanc, the tallest mountain in the French Alps, from the upstairs master bedroom. There is snow on it year-round.

Mountain climbers from all over the world come to climb it. My home's floor plan is open—the kitchen, eating area, and sitting room are one large room. In general, from the outside it is modern."

"Do you have a picture?" Angelina asked.

"No, I don't. I travel light and carry only what is necessary for the job at hand. But I can tell you more. It has many windows that bring in the morning sunshine. I have many houseplants. Upstairs, there is the master bedroom and one other bedroom I use as my office. The walls display many of my photographs. It is a small but warm and comfortable house. You could probably put my house into your bedroom at the palace. But it's near one of France's major ski villages—have you skied before?"

Angelina shook her head. "No, I haven't. I am willing to learn though. If you could teach me, that would be great. I have seen movies of people skiing. It looks like fun, and skiing with you, I know it will be." She paused and looked around. "It is getting late in the afternoon. We have just a little more shopping to do and get these musical instruments. I can tell my security team is getting nervous and wants us to get back to the villa. No bike riding on this trip."

"Let us go and finish our shopping," I said. "It has been fun today hanging around with you in this village of Pak Nhai. Did your security team check out the bathrooms before you enter the room at Colonel Gorky's villa?"

"In some cases, they will do that," Angelina replied. "When I am with my mother, a female bodyguard will certainly check everything. How would you like to be my bodyguard?"

I smiled. "I thought I was," I said as I showed her my pistol. "Well, I would enjoy that responsibility. Can I sleep with you too?"

Angelina laughed. "You always have an answer for everything. I can't wait to get to the palace. I need a warm bath. Since you're my bodyguard, will you bathe me?"

"Let's go," I replied. Moments later at the central market area, I said, "Oh, these instruments are very special. I like them. Are these the primitive musical instruments you purchased?"

"Yes, aren't they great?" Angelina replied. "They come from a Montagnard village not too far from here."

"What a great find. I am happy to get these for your bedroom, but what about your parents' gifts? We need to find something for your parents. What are we going to tell Colonel Gorky if we show up with nothing?"

"I will tell Colonel Gorky that you are my parents' gift," Angelina said. "What is he going to say? Nothing! He knows my parents have everything." She smiled at me, then continued. "It will be delightful to have you running around the palace. I might be jealous of my mother. She loves France, and, well, you are from France. I have a big advantage over her though—I am younger and in love with you."

A Montagnard man playing a bamboo musical instrument.

"With all the security around your palace and checking on you all the time, how can we sleep together at night?" I asked. "I am a stranger there, and they will be watching. Do you have any ideas?"

"My mother will probably place you next to my bedroom," Angelina replied. "I have a door that connects the rooms. I will unlock the door from my side and you unlock the door from your side. We will be safe to play all night, but you must go to your room before seven a.m. We will relock our doors then. When the maids and servants are going around checking on things, they will think we slept in our rooms alone. Now, let's get back. I want to be given a bath. I am sticky from today's heat."

CHAPTER 23
Princess Bopha Sovannar

We returned to the villas, and the security team was relieved to be back.

Colonel Gorky met us as dinner was being prepared. Bopha had put the meal together for us most of the day. She was anxious for us to try her meal. It was one of Cambodia's traditional foods. You have to eat the food with your fingers. This would be interesting for me.

As all of us, except Bopha, gathered around the table, a server brought the food to the table. Even the colonel was surprised by the appearance and presentation. Primitive flute music played in the background, and the servers were dressed in their native clothing.

Bopha came from the kitchen and danced around the table to the flute music. Her dancing was seductive around the colonel's chair. It was quite a show. We clapped and cheered as she finished her dancing.

After, we began our meal. A server gave each of us a towel drenched in lemon juice to clean our hands after each of the seven courses. There was food I had never tasted before; my taste buds salivated for each course.

We were told that Bopha had worked on this meal all day. We all told Bopha at the end of the meal how spectacular the presentation was and the choice of food.

"Instead of Bopha modeling, maybe she should be a chef on Lake Geneva," I whispered to the colonel.

Colonel Gorky smiled but said, "No, I need her here with me. Bopha is very helpful in my surroundings. She helps the chef in purchasing food and organizing the staff when I have guests from different countries. She is very clever at coming up with menus for our kitchen staff and entertainment staff. Without her by my side, I would have to spend too much time in these areas instead of on my military duties." Colonel Gorky then rose from his chair. "If you will excuse me, I must work on my business for Angelina's father's meeting. Once again, Bopha, the dinner was delicious, and my hands have never been so clean before."

All of us laughed and nodded in agreement.

The servants cleaned off the table and took the dishes to the kitchen. Angelina and I went for a walk outside to see the moon. Unfortunately, it was cloudy. However, the lighted compound made it easy to see.

We managed to walk down to the boat dock to see if any riverboats might be passing by. We sat down for a while, waiting—or should I say, hugging each other passionately. If Queen Mary came by, we wouldn't have noticed. Neither of us could stand this foreplay, so we scurried off to her villa. After closing her windows from possible viewers, Angelina underdressed and fetched washcloths from the bathroom.

I quickly removed my clothing and asked, "Can we take a shower together instead?"

"This will be exciting," Angelina replied, "I will enjoy taking a shower with you. You can clean my body with your lemon hands, Jean Claude!"

"I am ready for our shower."

Angelina laughed. "You are ready for something else by the looks of your body. I must train your body to be more patient. I don't know from experience but I can tell you are strong. My mother told me about the male body but you are different from those stories."

I said, "What did your mother say?"

"I can't tell you everything! I would be embarrassed. The things my mother told me are lady talk. I can tell you this: you have a very interesting body. I have looked forward to this day. The way you move so softly, strongly, and slowly with your hands. I can feel your love for me. When we are close, my feelings move me closer to you. It's difficult to explain, but I love it. My mother never talked about this with me. She never mentioned the different ways you can be kissed." Angelina walked over to me. "These romantic moments drive me crazy. I want more and more of you. I just can't stand the emotional desire I have for you to be inside me. I dream of us in my sleep. I will have you repeatedly in my dreams until I physically have you inside me."

"Angelina, I must tell you something," I replied. "I have left a lovely lady back in France, she was born in Norway. Her name is Sofie, and I haven't seen or talked to her in months. I left her to come here and report about the war." I set the stage just in case I made the mistake of saying Sofie's name during one of these hot, passionate interludes with Angelina. I felt terrible but I had to be honest with Angelina—I didn't have a choice but to play along with my mission.

"Now look at me—in the Presidential Palace with the prince of Laos's daughter. But I must stay focused on the reason why I am here. I must continue to write about the war over here in Vietnam, about Colonel Gorky's missions to unite the north with the south." I paused before continuing. "You have come into my life like a typhoon hitting an island. The power of love and emotions has set my heart on fire. I want you to love me in the way you have these past few days forever."

"I am shocked to hear your statement about this woman in France," Angelina finally replied. "I am jealous, but at the same time, you are beautiful and I don't blame her for loving you. Jean Claude, do you miss her?"

"Yes, I do," I said honestly. "We have strong feelings for each other and great harmony."

"Don't tell me any more about her!" Angelina exclaimed. "We are here and together *today*. This is our world here, and we are insulated from the rest of the world."

I nodded. "Yes, of course."

Angelina continued. "Jean Claude, you will need a few things before we meet my parents, but I know where to get them—my father goes to a few stores in Vientiane. We will talk about that later though, once we have a chance to make plans for shopping. You and I will have fun traveling around my city together. And we will put the musical instruments on the wall in my bedroom."

I smiled. "Will your parents care if I am in your bedroom?"

"No," Angelina said, "my parents are too busy with the day-to-day duties, and having Colonel Gorky there, my father will be busy with his group and meetings all day. We will have the palace to ourselves. But we can't be noisy in our bedrooms and draw attention."

"I can't wait. We should get some rest for the trip tomorrow morning. Does your staff know I am coming with you?"

"Yes, and they asked if you needed help packing your things for the trip. I told them you didn't have too much to pack. Everyone will be ready to leave after breakfast. I can't wait for us to leave. Vientiane will come alive when you and I arrive and visit all the interesting places around the city. Jean Claude, this is like a dream—you might have to pinch me so I can wake up! Now, kiss me!"

I did and then asked, "Do you think we should ask your mother to come with us occasionally? I don't want her to feel shut out of our activities while I am there as a visitor. Maybe lunch on the river, or we could take her on a boat lunch cruise. What do you think?"

Angelina smiled. "I was thinking the same thing. We have a yacht and a crew that will serve us lunch. Having my mother along would be wonderful. She hasn't been on this type of cruise before with just a family group. I don't know about the security for us, but her staff will work out the details. Good suggestion, Jean Claude, we are beginning to think similarly."

"Let's go to bed," I said. "I have a bedtime story to tell you."

Angelina laughed. "Jean Claude, you are too funny. Hey, what are you doing?"

"Thinking about us on the yacht. Someday I would like to take you upstream, way up into China to explore the small villages along the way, learn about their cultures, and write about our adventure. We could print a picture book about this special trip we would have."

Angelina sighed. "I like this bedtime story. Oh, Jean Claude, you put me into a love trance. Words cannot explain my feelings at this moment. I never want to lose these moments with you. I hope my parents kidnap you. I'll hide you in my bedroom."

Finally, we settled down for the night and fell asleep on top of the bed.

CHAPTER 24
THE PALACE

After we ate and said our good-byes, we got our luggage and loaded it into the jeeps to head to the helicopter pad for take-off. I turned to wave at the palace staff standing in the distance. I would likely be going on combat missions with them when I returned.

We strapped ourselves into our seats and began lift-off. Our helicopter was full of clothing trunks, security staff, cooking staff, and servers. I looked back and noticed two faces on the young servers who looked scared to death. It must be their first time on a helicopter.

Angelina and I held hands for the whole trip to Vientiane. The trip wasn't long, about one hour. The helicopter landed at the back of the palace. We could see from the air a narrow red carpet where we were going to land.

Colonel Gorky's helicopter was first to land. Our helicopter landed on the red carpet away from Colonel Gorky's for security reasons. The prince and his wife were there to greet all of us as we disembarked from the helicopters. Palace staff and military personnel waited to greet us until we were clear from the helicopter blades. I must have looked like hell—everyone else was wearing dresses and suits and I looked like I came out of the battlefield. I planned to look for more presentable clothing later.

I made my way over to Prince Vongkhamchanh and his wife, who seemed anxious to meet me and hug their daughter. They received me with cordial warmth, and Mrs. Vongkhamchanhr kissed me on the cheek. This was a very nice start to my relationship with her.

After greeting everyone, we moved into the ballroom. It was the size of a football field.

What the hell am I doing here? I asked myself. I should be in the jungles of Laos, Cambodia, and Vietnam, getting intel and reporting back to Nha Trang. Yet here I was at the Presidential Palace, escorting the prince of Laos's daughter. Not only escorting the prince of Laos's daughter but sleeping with her! I could have my head cut off and nobody would know.

The prince and his wife had a small buffet that filled three tables. Fresh fruit, cold juices, and roasted chicken meat on a stick for the personnel who came from Colonel Gorky's compound.

Colonel Gorky and Bopha brought with them a case of French wine. I brought three primitive musical instruments, which brought some interest. The prince and his wife liked them. Angelina's mother wanted to know more about their origin, and Angelina shared the background with her mother.

Colonel Gorky and his three officers joined the prince in another room while I stayed with Angelina and her mother.

"How long will you stay with us, Monsieur Martin?" Mrs. Vongkhamchanh asked.

"I will be returning to Cambodia with Colonel Gorky and his staff once his business is finished with your husband," I replied. "Colonel Gorky has told me about three days."

"I will ask tomorrow when all of you are rested," Mrs. Vongkhamchanh said. "Monsieur Martin, I will show you to your room during your stay. I hope you find it comfortable and restful. Angelina can point out to you where everything is and how all the plumbing works, the phone system, how security will be walking the hallways, and where to go if you need a light meal during the night."

"Mrs. Vongkhamchanh, I want to explain that I am overwhelmed by your invitation to come here with your beautiful daughter," I said. "I was very surprised to see her at Colonel Gorky's villa when I arrived with the troops from the north. I was sent to the kitchen to get a bottle of wine, and Angelina was standing there, waiting for me. A beautiful shining star. I was at a loss for words. I can tell you, Mrs. Vongkhamchanh, I melted; my heart fell with happiness and joy."

I continued. "I carried your daughter's friendliness with me for several months. When I got to Colonel Gorky's compound and was invited to have dinner that evening, I was caught off-guard by Angelina's presence. What a gift; I couldn't believe my eyes. I was very happy to meet her again. At that time, I didn't even know her name. Mrs. Vongkhamchanh, I thank you for raising a responsible, enjoyable, loving daughter. I come from a simple family of farmers. I was raised in the French Alps, Haute-Savoie. I have seen many things from a young age. I respect life and how important it is to live each day concerning our existence. In your role here in the Presidential Palace, the optics you show to your people are extremely important. Angelina has told me that you and your husband are the guiding light of her life. With my brief acquaintance with you, I can see what Angelina was talking about. You are a special person, who cares for others. I want to court your daughter with the highest degree of integrity."

Mrs. Vongkhamchanh smiled warmly. "Jean Claude, I welcome you into our home with open hands. You can count on our daughter to extend our hospitality while staying here. My husband and I would like to dine with you and Angelina alone before you return with Colonel Gorky. The prince and I want to offer you protection while in Vientiane as well. Angelina and you are welcome to use the yacht, the main kitchen, and Angelina knows other places you can have access to. The prince also has a medal of honor to award you for your bravery here in Laos with the drug cartel."

I inclined my head in thanks. "It would be my pleasure to visit with you and your husband. I would also love to interview the two of you. It would be very exciting reading for the readers of my newspaper back in France. I hear from Colonel Gorky that your husband could be the future president of Laos. This must be very electrifying to your family. If this comes about, may I still visit you?"

"Jean Claude, I will have your room ready for you always!" Mrs. Vongkhamchanh replied. "I will have your name put on the door!"

"Oh, Mother, put both of our names on the door!" Angelina interjected.

Mrs. Vongkhamchanh eyed her daughter. "You are moving too fast, Angelina. Jean Claude has to agree and be willing to stay with us in the palace. It will be a big change for both of you. No matter what, your security will be your father's concern. Nobody knows for sure what will happen here in Laos. Maybe my husband will not be president and we will live the life as we do today in Vientiane."

"Mother, it doesn't matter what life we live," Angelina said. "To me, it's the quality that matters. I think Jean Claude agrees. You and my father have worked in the diplomatic arena your whole lives. I want us to be happy in whatever role we have. Jean Claude is a war correspondent going off in a few days. We might not see him again."

I grasped Angelina's hand and said, "Please, let's move on to what is happening now. I love you. Live today like no tomorrow."

Mrs. Vongkhamchanh nodded her head. "I agree with Jean Claude. Angelina, I know the burning feelings you have for Jean Claude. When I first met your father in France, I felt a gripping desire. When you fall into true love, your heart knows the difference. I am pleased to hear you talk about love and the deep feelings you have. But remember, you are both young. I am asking you to develop your love. If it is true love, we will accept this relationship. Your father must approve this arrangement, and I think it is too soon to ask him. Let's enjoy ourselves, have fun, and improve our relationships. I must leave you for now and join the prince."

Angelina turned to me after her mother left. "Let us go to our rooms and see the layout. I hope we can unlock the doors between our two rooms. Do you see the big door over there?"

I nodded. "Yes, I will try unlocking my door."

"I will go to my room and see if my door can be unlocked," Angelina replied.

Yes, these doors were opened for our pleasure.

Oh boy, can't wait to see what will happen when all of us retire for the night, I thought to myself.

As we looked around Angelina's bedroom walls to find a place to hang the primitive musical instruments, there was an announcement made over the loudspeakers about having lunch in the garden in one hour. Angelina and I had a little time to ourselves to get ready. After the flight, we felt as if a quick shower would be delightful. We got undressed and took a shower. *I could get used to this, and to hell with everything else.*

I thought about Lieutenant Colonel Miller in Nha Trang. What would he think about me now? I smiled inside just thinking about all the training I received to get here. All I really needed was to be a good lover.

Lieutenant Colonel Miller had told me to find a safe house in Laos or Cambodia. Well, I chose Laos. *This is the best safe house I could find, Lieutenant Colonel Miller.* However, I needed to be careful in my relaxed surroundings not to say things about my true past. My life would be over. I couldn't think about this because my feelings for Angelina were deep. If she found out, it would destroy her emotionally. *Stay focused, you are a spy looking for information to pass on that will save American lives in South Vietnam and curb the military strategy actions of North Vietnam.*

We hurried and got dressed and rushed to the garden for lunch.

I managed to go around with Angelina introducing myself. Most of the attendees spoke Laotian from the ethnic group of Hmong and had a thick accent. Angelina helped me with the translation. I relaxed during my lunch, despite being surrounded by these diplomats from different regions in Laos. There was food on the tables I had never seen before. I passed by them and moved to food I would enjoy eating. Angelina and I looked at each other and smiled. She knew about my tastes in food from her visit to Cambodia.

"Angelina, I need to find a bathroom. Can you assist me?" I whispered to her at one point.

"I will show you when you are ready to leave," Angelina replied. "I must tell my mother about your request for a bathroom. She will laugh but I shall join you—I need the bathroom too."

"Please ask your mother what restroom to use!"

CHAPTER 25
THE PILE OF MAPS

Angelina and I whisked away from the garden and went into her father's office. As I walked by his desk, I noticed a stack of maps. On top was a map of Nha Trang written in bold lettering. The maps could be the plans for the attack on Têt. Looking up at the wall, I noticed a CCTV camera and continued to follow Angelina into the bathroom.

After a while, we returned to the luncheon with smiles on our faces.

"What took you two so long to return?" Mrs. Vongkhamchanh asked coyly.

Angelina scoffed. "Mother, we had to kiss each other before coming back. I needed Jean Claude to relax. Can't you see his smile? His eyes are going around in circles."

The three of us laughed.

We finished lunch in the garden and had time for ourselves. Angelina wanted to take me to the Mekong River, where her father's yacht was located, so we could take a short boat ride on the river. She asked her mother if this was possible. Her mother approved and had one of the staff members decide for us.

We met up with Colonel Gorky and I shared with him about the boat trip on the Mekong River. He was concerned about the possibility of river pirates taking over Angelina's security and kidnapping her, so Colonel Gorky gave me his pistol. I was surprised he would do such a thing. I thanked him and reassured him I would return the pistol when we got back to the palace.

On the way to the dock, I noticed a man watching me very carefully. I thought he might be my handler in this city. While we were getting out of the vehicle I gave the possible handler a secret code, and he responded with his code. I didn't have any intel to give him at this time. He was probably thinking about what I was going to do with the prince of Laos's daughter. I got on the boat with her security team, and we went upstream.

As the boat went along, I could see a park, which was located very close to the palace. I could easily walk there and I decided I would ask if I could go there during my stay.

While the boat struggled upstream, I saw other boats on the Mekong delivering goods to different locations on the river. People on other boats passing by viewed our boat with curiosity.

Finally, we made it to our upriver destination and turned around.

Mekong riverboats busy going up and down the river.
Vientiane, Laos

Fishing village on the Mekong River, south of Vientiane, Laos.

Going downstream was like floating on a cloud. But I still couldn't stop thinking about the maps in the prince's office. How could I get access to his office without being seen? Would Colonel Gorky bring these maps to his villa in Cambodia? I decided I needed to keep my eyes on the office during my stay. I thought of putting a secret camera at the entrance of his office so I could get pictures of anyone going into his office. This could be risky though. I decided to wait and see what tomorrow brings.

That evening, Angelina and I had a light meal in the kitchen while the prince and other guests, like Colonel Gorky, had a formal dinner. I was content having a private meal with Angelina in the kitchen. After we ate, Angelina wanted to go up to our bedroom and play cards.

Morning came early and we were playing around the two bedrooms. I tried to be as quiet as possible but we couldn't stop playing with each other and making sounds that I was sure could be heard in other rooms.

"There isn't anybody else in this wing of the palace," Angelina whispered in my ear. "My mother must trust you with me. Only VIPs stay in this section of the palace."

I was pleased and comforted to hear this. I needed to keep her mother's trust.

Breakfast time came too quickly and we had to get ready and go downstairs to join other guests. I was in the bathroom shaving when Angelina came in and announced that she wanted to shave me. I was expecting her to shave my facial hair, but instead, she moved to my lower area and shaved me clean.

"Why are you shaving that area of my body?" I asked.

"You'll see tonight," Angelina replied.

We finished getting ready for breakfast, but it was hard to stop Angelina's actions. She wanted to go back to bed and play around. I insisted we go downstairs because it was not the best time. With a disappointed look from Angelina, we scurried downstairs.

We arrived just barely on time. All the main guests were at the table waiting to be served. Colonel Gorky and Bopha arrived after and sat down beside us. We talked about our activities yesterday and what we did in the evening before going to bed. We discussed what could happen today and where the main action was going to be.

"I might have a chance to go visit the French Embassy this morning with Angelina," I said. "I want to show her off and tell them where I have been and when I might be going back to your compound, Colonel Gorky. You had mentioned something about me going on missions with one or two of your main commanding officers. Is this still an option?"

"Jean Claude, we have to wait and see," Colonel Gorky replied. "Major Tran has some plans for me right after we return. I must go with him. I don't know how long this gathering will take. If you want to go with us, you are welcome. I will have a better idea when we return to my compound."

"Great, I would like to come with you. Maybe there is a story."

"I don't know what Major Tran has to say about this," Colonel Gorky said. "We will find out once we get back to Pak Nhai."

MY YEARS AS A WAR CORRESPONDENT

Everyone began eating and continued talking about nothing of import. Angelina touched my thigh with her left hand. I looked at her and gave a sexy smile. She snickered and smiled at me. *What does she have in store for us tonight?* I thought to myself.

When breakfast ended, the other guests went to the prince's office. Angelina and I went up to our bedrooms and got ready to walk to the embassy. Of course, we had to play around for a while before going to the embassy.

Inside the French Embassy, we met different personnel who worked there. I saw my handler, and he introduced himself as Mr. Tong. He asked several questions about my trip to Pak Nhai and what working with Colonel Gorky at his compound was like. Mr. Tong then wanted to know how I met Angelina and how long I had known her.

Angelina stepped into the conversation before I could answer and told this man that we met when she was in Hanoi at a banquet party. After she finished, I asked, "Mr. Tong, Could I use your office for a moment? I need to write some stories that must be sent to France. I will reimburse this office for any materials used."

My real plan was to leave the reports for Mr. Tong on top of his typewriter for a quick and safe location. Mr. Tong knew the importance of my being here and would return to his office immediately after we left. In the reports, I had detailed information about tunnel-making

My handler, Mr. Tong, at the French Embassy in Vientiane, Laos.

equipment coming from Russia, also the up-and-coming Tết celebration and military planning from Colonel Gorky's office, a map I drew which showed Nha Trang. I warned the handler in the report that this information must be rushed to Nha Trang today and to get all the American encampments ready for attacks on Tết.

"Jean Claude, I can't let Angelina go with you to the back offices," Mr. Tong said. "She will have to stay here."

"That will be fine with me," Angelina said. "Jean Claude, how long will you be?"

"It shouldn't take long," I told her. "I have made short notes for the stories. It will be quick for me to finish them. Is there anything else you would like to see?"

Angelina smiled. "No, Jean Claude. I have been here before, when my parents and I visited France. You know my father is a citizen of France."

I nodded. "I remember you telling me."

Afterward, I left the embassy relieved. Having the perfect chance to meet Mr. Tong, turning over the intel, and getting these reports back to Nha Trang left me feeling like the weight of the world came off my shoulders. I could go back to making Angelina happy tonight.

As we walked toward a pharmacy to get some cream for my wound, Angelina pointed out to me that there was a medical store across the street.

"Jean Claude, I need to tell you that I am sore from our lovemaking," Angelina said. "This is the reason I shaved you this morning. I would like to play with you and see what it is like to get a man excited. I am anxious to try. Give me a day to heal. Jean Claude, can we try this tonight?"

"Why wait for tonight?" I joked.

"Let's see what happens from this experiment," Angelina replied.

"After we finish with the shower," I began, "I will give you a massage. With great care for your soreness, I will touch you like a feather."

Angelina smiled. "I'll race you back."

"Oh no, don't race back; save our energy."

Angelina nodded. "All right, we won't race back—but walk at a faster pace than we are walking now. Jean Claude, I won't let you leave in two days. What am I going to do? It has been an experience that will stay with me forever. I keep telling myself that you will come back for me. But what if you don't? Where can I find you? My heart is sure you will come back for me. I trust my heart but I struggle with my mind."

I grabbed her hands. "I wish upon us that our love for each other continues to be strong. I do think about you and how you touch me, making me feel great about myself—how you seduce me, giving me the path to love you—and I can't live with the idea of you making love with another man. I hate to think about these things. When I was coming down to Colonel Gorky's compound, I didn't know I would ever see you again. I would close my eyes and pretend to make love with you. Angelina, let us go upstairs for playtime."

"Are you ready?" Angelina asked. "I will check with my mother and tell her we are going upstairs and resting for a while. She will be understanding and might think that your leg is bothering you."

I smiled. "Which leg?"

We checked in with Angelina's mother and she told us that in the afternoon around three, she was having a small gathering of people for an afternoon luncheon and wanted us to join.

Angelina replied for both of us. "We will attend. Do you need any help getting the luncheon organized?"

"No, the servers and I will get everything ready," Mrs. Vongkhamchanh said. "It will be just a few people coming. I would appreciate your presence when it is time to receive the guests and place them at their tables."

Angelina and I nodded our heads in agreement. We then went upstairs, got undressed, and ran toward the shower. Both of us were excited to have the time to play. I could go into all the exotic details, but I will leave it to you and your imagination of what went on between us.

When we were finished, Angelina and I got dressed and went downstairs to meet the guests for the luncheon. The luncheon was attended by Colonel Gorky and his staff, members of the prince's inner circle, and other individuals from different locations around the city.

After the luncheon, Angelina and I asked her mother if we could take a short ride to the Mekong River shoreline on bicycles. We went riding and had to take two security personnel with us. Security staff would likely be happy when I left the palace.

All the while, I was thinking of getting my hands on the map of Nha Trang. I hadn't seen them since the first day here. How could I take photos of these maps? I was running out of time, for the lunar new year was in five months.

Due to all the meetings here in the palace, I feared it would happen. My only chance was to find a path at the Pak Nhai compound. Colonel Gorky would have a close eye on these maps. He had security cameras in his office and the hall. But just maybe, I could be present with him during a training exercise for these attacks around the major cities in South Vietnam. Wouldn't that be lucky? I could write news articles about these attacks before they even happened.

Once Colonel Gorky's military plans were set in motion, I would release the articles about Khe Sanh Valley attack on January 21. I would also suggest that the news articles on Saigon and Nha Trang be released on January 31 to Colonel Gorky, if he told me anything about the lunar new year attacks or if I had a moment to ask him. Right now, he didn't know I was aware of the maps.

I was told by Colonel Gorky's staff that we were leaving the palace tomorrow afternoon for the Pak Nhai compound. My vacation here was over. I had to get back into the newspaper mission. Being with Angelina had deadened my drive to get out there and fight for our military in South Vietnam.

CHAPTER 26
Going to Pak Nhai, Cambodia

I was the last one in line as the prince and Mrs. Vongkhamchanh said their warm and friendly goodbyes to each of us. When it came to me, Mrs. Vongkhamchanh kissed me on my cheek.

"Jean Claude, you will always have an invite to the palace," Prince Vongkhamchanh said. "Angelina and you appear to be in love. One day, I would like to sit down and talk with you about your feelings toward Angelina. I apologize for not finding time to talk with you on this trip. But I have a feeling that you will be back to see us soon. If you need a helicopter ride in and around Laos, just go to one of our government offices and they will call my office. Arrangements will be made for you. Angelina and some security personnel will come and get you."

"This generous invite will help me get back here and spend valuable time with Angelina, Mrs. Vongkhamchanh, and you, sir," I replied. "I appreciate the invitation. I had a memorable visit, and this will be carried in my mind and heart forever."

"Here is a list of telephone numbers you can use to call," Angelina said. "Please, Jean Claude, I need you to call me often."

I held her hand and said, "I will see you very soon. I love you. Angelina, you will always be in my heart. I will return, Angelina!"

Angelina deserved an explanation, but I couldn't tell her the truth about my missions; it was easier to tell her nothing at all.

Soon, I would fly in a private helicopter, have a delicious meal, and tomorrow I would likely kill a man. What a screwed-up world I lived in. I needed to concentrate and force my mind back to my missions.

After Angelina and I kissed goodbye, I joined the others near the helicopter pad. We climbed aboard, and the helicopter took off toward the Pak Nhai compound with the colonel and his staff.

There was another man with us I had never met before. I kept watching him with curiosity. I was sure Colonel Gorky would introduce him to me once we got to the compound. I fell into a dreamy state, reviewing my stay with Angelina's parents as well as the entire trip. It was like a dream a person might have after reading a book about Indochina back in its heyday.

After we landed at the compound, Colonel Gorky wanted me to carry some rolled-up maps—the same ones from the palace.

"Colonel Gorky, there're so many rolls of maps," I said. "I'll leave my personal belongings and carry these maps to your office."

"Jean Claude, give your bag to one of my staff," Colonel Gorky replied. "They will take your things to your room. These maps must not be unattended. You must not let anyone look at them. Come, I will show you where to place them in my office."

I followed the colonel to his office and laid down the maps on his desk. The colonel put them into a safe built behind his bookshelf.

After that, we went into the kitchen and helped Bopha get our lunch on the veranda. All through lunch, I couldn't stop thinking about the maps and how important they were for me to record. How could I get access to them?

After lunch, the colonel and Bopha went to their room, and I had the opportunity to walk around the compound. I returned to the medical clinic with gifts for Ms. Sing, the nurse who dressed my wounds, and the doctor. I had over-purchased medical supplies in Vientiane, and I didn't need them anymore. I went into the clinic waiting room to see if Ms. Sing and the doctor were there. I saw Ms. Sing and she was surprised to see me again.

"I have a small gift for you and the doctor who sewed me up," I told her.

"Thank you," Ms. Sing said in French, "for the needed medical items. I will tell the doctor that you have been thinking about us. He isn't here right now but will return in a few days."

The two of us walked down to the river. Along the way to the river, she told me about her life and where she went to nursing school. She missed being around other people her age and was pleased to have me around to talk with her. Out of curiosity, I asked what her full name was. She was glad to write her first name, "Sing," and her last name, "Keona Malaythong," on a piece of paper. Once Sing and I returned to the clinic, I wandered back to the Colonel's villa where I met Bopha sunbathing on the veranda.

"Jean Claude, you look lost and in love with Angelina," Bopha said. "You miss her, don't you?"

"I can't stand being without Angelina and not having her by my side," I replied. "We have a lovable harmony between us. Yes, I miss her."

"I can call Angelina and she will come," Bopha said. "You appear a little lovesick. She can bring your spirit back. Maybe you will feel better later. Colonel Gorky mentioned that you could go on a mission in two days. It's too short for Angelina to come and spend time with you. Once you return, Angelina could visit. It would put you back up into the clouds again. You will need her when you come back from the field mission."

I nodded. "Sometimes, I can feel Angelina touch me. Her hands are so soft and feathery. If you talk with her while I am away, please tell her I think about her and love her. I am looking forward to seeing her again soon. Do you know if the colonel will talk with me about this trip today?"

Bopha shook her head. "I don't know his plans, but he is having a meeting with Major Tran right now. He was looking for you to go with him. The guards told him you were at the boat dock with the medical clinic nurse. Are you having problems with your leg?"

"No, I just had to talk to someone," I replied. "I miss Angelina very much and we had many lovely moments at her boat dock. I looked for you but I didn't find you in my search and I came across Ms. Sing walking to the medical clinic."

"The colonel will be returning for a late afternoon lunch," Bopha said. I am preparing a great luncheon menu and I want you to join us. Would you enjoy eating with us?"

"Yes, I would enjoy the pleasure of your company and tasting your food again. However, what if the colonel invites Major Tran for lunch? They might continue talking about their meeting and I don't think they will want me around while discussing their matters."

"Oh, Jean Claude, you are family," Bopha replied. "The colonel doesn't talk about military issues around me either. If Major Tran joins us, you can join us at the table. You will have a chance to see Major Tran differently, other than in combat."

"Okay, we'll wait and see what the colonel has planned. I'm sure he will let you know if Major Tran will join him for lunch."

"Yes, we'll see what the colonel's plans are," Bopha said, "but either way, you are invited by me. So, can I expect you for lunch?"

"Yes, thank you," I replied.

"See you later for lunch."

CHAPTER 27
INTO SOUTH VIETNAM

I went off to my room and I looked around at my things. I had been goofing off and needed to get back into the combat readiness mood.

With Têt coming up, I needed to get photos of the maps so the American forces had time to get ready for these attacks around South Vietnam. I wondered what Colonel Gorky would think about having stories already written and on his desk about the attacks before they happened. I would explain to the colonel that since there would be so many battles throughout South Vietnam, getting the story told as it happened would take too much time. The colonel could instead send the articles out when each battle happened. The only thing we needed was photographs.

This whole campaign was Colonel Gorky's military strategy for total victory in South Vietnam. Could I sell this idea to the colonel? I was fighting with time. I needed the right timing to ask him. Perhaps I could be with him at a meeting with his staff officers. I would then ask if I could speak about the news coverage of these attacks and how important it would be to let the world view these engagements around South Vietnam over the lunar new year. This news in American homes would be very powerful, which was an avenue Colonel Gorky had told me before: "Get the bad news into the living rooms of American homes." This vehicle of news reporting could be the straw that broke the camel's back. I thought I had a good chance of convincing the colonel. I just had to get my hands on these maps.

"Lunch is ready and the colonel is here," Bopha called to me.

"I am coming," I called back.

"Jean Claude, Bopha told me you are getting ready to go out on a mission?" Colonel Gorky said at lunch. "First, I must explain to you that the mission will be very dangerous and could cause many casualties on both sides. After we have lunch, I will take you to my office and show you the details of this mission."

"I want to see what you have planned for this mission," I replied, "where we will be going, and what type of resistance we could encounter as well as who might be fighting us and what strength they could oppose us."

"Let us eat and enjoy our meal," Bopha interjected.

We had lunch and Colonel Gorky asked a server to have Lieutenant Colonel Pham, Major Tran, and Captain Duc meet us in his office.

In his office, all of us sat around Colonel Gorky's conference desk and waited for the colonel to arrive. When he did, we all stood up and waited for the colonel to sit down.

Colonel Gorky said, "Please be seated." Then he continued, "For those of you who haven't met Jean Claude Martin, I will take this time to introduce you to him. Jean Claude represents a French newspaper, *La Combat-Haute-Savoie*. Jean Claude is a proven combat field person. He has been in two hand-to-hand combative attacks. Major Tran was a witness to the last attack. I trust him and I am asking all my staff to respect his presence in my command. I have been told that Laos and North Vietnam's commanding officers share the same sentiment. Does anyone in this room have anything to say currently about Jean Claude before we move on to the issue at hand?"

Colonel Gorky waited for a response, but none came. "Okay, we must talk about the up-and-coming lunar new year attacks. I have put in front of you an agenda for us to stay on track this afternoon: First, are the supply trails into the areas we want to attack ready and being supplied? Second, is the manpower sufficient in place for these selected cities in South Vietnam? Third, will there be medical clinics available during and after the conflict? Fourth, are the escape routes open for the able soldiers to use? And finally, do we have safe houses for moving the dead and seriously wounded in place? I want to go around the table and hear your responses to these questions. Before that though—Jean Claude, would you come with me for a moment?"

"Yes, I will," I replied.

I followed the colonel to another room where he began explaining he would be speaking in Vietnamese. After the meeting, he continued, he would explain to me what the conclusions were from each member of the meeting and he wanted me to reply to him after dinner.

When I left the meeting, I joined Bopha in another room off the veranda. We talked about her country, and she gave me some ideas about writing stories. It would be a chance to see her family and write about them one day. But Bopha didn't know what was going to happen after the war, and neither did I.

I explained to Bopha about wanting to get through the present before writing about the future of Indochina later. Maybe one day the world would see Indochina evolve into one country.

We walked around the compound for a while before Bopha had to decide for dinner.

I continued to walk around the compound just for some exercise and went down to the river to watch the boats. One of Colonel Gorky's aides came and told me the meeting was over and to return to his villa.

Soon, we were sitting down for dinner. "Let's eat!" Colonel Gorky called. He then turned to me and said, "Jean Claude, you and I will sit down outside on the veranda and discuss what plans will be put into motion very soon."

We ate another delicious meal that Bopha had prepared for us. But I couldn't stop myself from missing Angelina. I would look at the chair she sat in while visiting the villa, wondering what she was doing and if she was thinking about me.

After finishing dinner, the colonel and I retired to the veranda.

"Jean Claude, what we discuss tonight will stay between us," Colonel Gorky said. "You can't write or tell anyone about the information I am going to discuss with you. It is a very secret plan. If there are any leaks about this secret information, you would be the first suspect. I have you in my confidence; I trust you. You will not discuss any operations within my network, how we do military tactics, supply chain, and how our forces get supplied into South Vietnam. Can you live with these conditions?"

"Yes, Colonel Gorky," I replied. "You have been very honest with me, guiding me from the beginning of the relationship. I have learned so much from being around you and the staff. Should we speak about these plans later if we are alone?"

"I don't want to talk about them," Colonel Gorky said, "for other ears might be nearby. I will approach you first. You can't imagine what is in store for you tonight. This is a very complicated undertaking. I have to lay the details out in order. There are two parts. The first part, I will tell you tonight. The second part will be discussed in my office tomorrow morning after breakfast."

CHAPTER 28
PART ONE

"Okay I will start with part one," Colonel Gorky began. "Most of our supplies are from the south. Food is grown by Viet Cong farmers and soldiers within the southern borders of Vietnam. Cambodia's seaports have roadways into South Vietnam for armory goods. And weapons are available on the black market. We put gasoline-soaked rags into place to fool the US Air Force so they think their bombs hit something of value. Our engineers put dimmed lighting under trucks, cut out small areas in tree trunks, and put flammable liquid inside. This provided light to move supplies and soldiers down the trails. This method worked and couldn't be seen from any aircraft overhead. We also cut overgrown vines from the water's edge so they would float downstream. These vines were very large and men were able to hide in them. The current then moves them down the rivers into South Vietnam or to our suppling center in that area."

Viet Cong soldiers would hide with military hardware in these large entanglement vines (indicated by red dots) and float downstream to South Vietnam locations.

Colonel Gorky continued. "The number of people used to keep the supply chain active is around ninety thousand drivers, vehicle mechanics, general laborers, engineers, infantry, and antiaircraft military personnel. I began this transfer into a massive development when I first came to Vietnam. With the assistance of the 559th Engineer Corps, Nguyen Cong Ho and I completely overhauled the roads, tracks, waterways, mountainous passes, and seaport locations. This ambitious task added up to about ten thousand miles. The overall program for this expansion—as well as carving out new trails for moving supplies by truck, putting into place missile sites, and the fuel pipelines—was significant. Each encampment had an infantry, engineers, laborers, and transportation motor pools. In 1966, around three hundred and fifty missile sites along the web of trails led into South Vietnam.

"Now for the big one: Cambodia. The Sihanouk Trail, seaport, roads, waterways, and small trails carved their way through Cambodia and into South Vietnam, supplying the complete southern half of South Vietnam. This country is very important in the overall supply chain. All types of military supplies shipped from North Vietnam would come into port at Sihanoukville. What was interesting to us was that ships were flying communist flags from the eastern-bloc countries, mainly China and Russia. This is a tremendous advantage for us. The supplies from North Vietnam have been pouring into our warehouses along the western borders of South Vietnam at a fast pace. The logistical support has been outstanding, and I must say it is a remarkable success for the Communist Vietnamese leadership."

"Colonel Gorky, I have witnessed some of your military strategies, as well as the network of trails coming down from the north, coupled with the Cambodia seaport supply link," I said. "Most of the warehouse placements come down the trails into South Vietnam. What about the American intelligence agents capturing your personnel and interrogating them?"

"The CIA has limited access to our operations here in Laos and Cambodia," Colonel Gorky answered. "Most of the information they have is ambiguous. All the personnel, laborers, farmers, and mules are schooled in interrogations. For example, the mules transport four to six tons of supplies each day down the trails. Through Laos and into central South Vietnam, thousands of mules will form a line—like a train—and will travel half-a-day's trip with their loads to the next warehouse. They will return that afternoon, making it a one-day journey. Another group of mules will continue moving the supplies to another warehouse location. This system of half-day deliveries works out well. These trails are small, about two to three meters wide, and only travelable by foot or bicycle. In larger villages and new villages, the paths are wider, about four to six meters—Just wide enough for passage on foot or bicycle, pack animals, animal-drawn carts, jeeps, and small trucks. Small trees and other vegetation cover most of the paths, so from the air, it is hard to detect there is a road.

"Cambodia—well, that is another story, Jean Claude. The Viet Cong use this country freely. The supplies move very easily and quickly. The South Vietnamese Special Forces numbered about fifteen thousand men. They are used to patrol the border between Cambodia and South Vietnam, most of them being Viet Cong. If they saw mules bring supplies into South Vietnam, they would turn their face. Viet Cong organized over one thousand mules to move supplies into Tây Ninh province, South Vietnam. The tonnage is staggering. The coastline of South Vietnam is wide open to infiltration by sea. About fifty different places along the coast are easy to anchor and unload supplies. Meanwhile, the CIA reports less than one ton per day. They have no idea of the tonnage."

A tributary of the Mekong River used as one of the many supply waterway networks.

Riverboats were used to move large amounts on the Mekong River near My Tho.

A riverboat on the Saigon River near Bien Hoa, South Vietnam, used to supply the Viet Cong.

Viet Cong riverway warehouses.

A riverboat on the Saigon River near Bien Hoa, South Vietnam, used to supply Viet Cong

A Viet Cong tunnel with underwater entry and exit leading to the small village supply house in the Mekong Delta region.

A staging dock was used for loading small boats to supply small warehouses in the Mekong Delta.

A staging dock in the Mekong River for small boats to travel to warehouses in the area.

A route used to move supplies in the Mekong tributaries.

Small boats were used to move supplies in the Mekong River basin.

Riverboats on the Saigon River were used to transport larger amounts of supplies.

Colonel Gorky continued. "The CIA report is incorrect. Some of the food, clothing, medicines, weapons, ammunition, mines, grenades, and other nonmilitary items are brought into South Vietnam via Cambodian channels. The CIA believes most of these products are fabricated within South Vietnam in the Tây Ninh province. We have farms along the Ho Chi Minh trails where Viet Cong farmers produce food products for their usage. A few farms are inside South Vietnam. They operate as farmers during the day and perform military missions at night. There is complex tunneling in and around these farms. We even have fake tunnels with old food supplies for the Americans to find."

Watering well with a secret tunnel in Tây Ninh province.

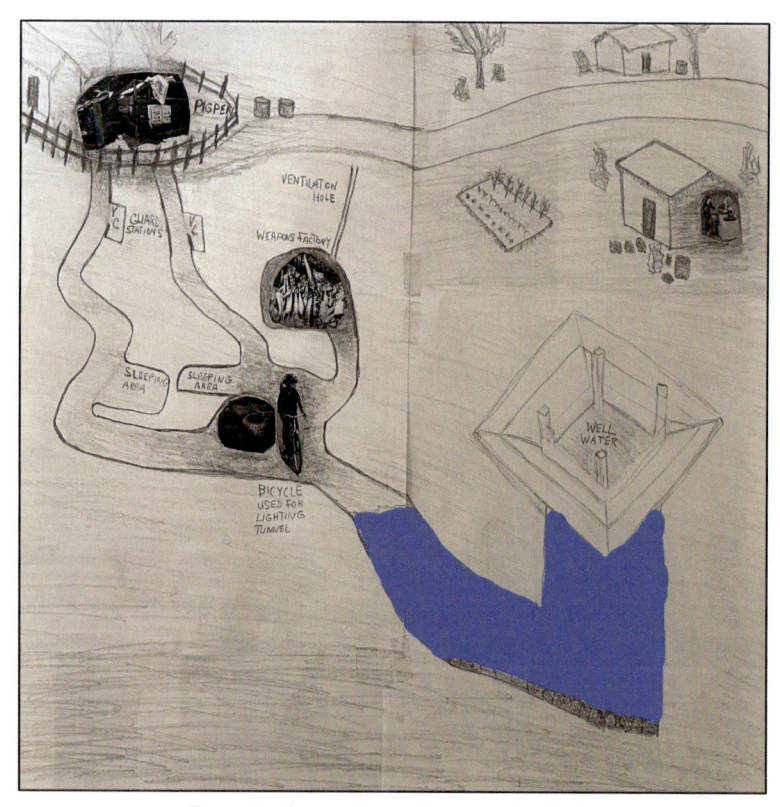

Example: A watering well was used to hide a small weapons factory near Tây Ninh province.

A Viet Cong farmer near Tây Ninh, South Vietnam.

Farms under Viet Cong control near the Cambodian border with South Vietnam.

Farmland controlled by Viet Cong in South Vietnam.

MY YEARS AS A WAR CORRESPONDENT

In the Tây Ninh region, a stone mountain tunnel complex and headquarters for the NVA and Viet Cong. The red lines indicate the path of the trail. The grass hasn't completely grown back.

Rice fields controlled by Viet Cong near Chau Doc in South Vietnam.

"As I hear from you," I said, "the American forces and its allies are using false intelligence for their planning to make their military strategy? I think getting intel from the POW who is caught in the field and interrogating them for information is ludicrous. Why don't the CIA and other branches of the intelligence community gather intel for their agency?"

175

"Where are they going to get these people to go out and get this type of intelligence? Nobody has the vision within the American forces intel group to take on this mission," Colonel Gorky replied.

"Can I speak to you openly about an idea that should have been tried?" I asked.

"Yes, you may. I want to hear what you have to say about this conflict we are in today."

I continued. "What if the American forces and its allies come to Vietnam, not with weapons and bombs, but ideas on how to make these countries productive? Use the formula applied in Japan after World War II: This plan put Japan on an industrial path—not only industrial theater but understructure, hospitals, schools, farm equipment, and the building of a stable government for its people. Could Indochina's people take on this task? I think about all the money spent on this war, all the civilians and soldiers of Indochina who have lost their lives or are lost in the vacuum of war. This conflict with military might isn't the answer for Indochina. The CIA is operating on 'let us see' and hopes the intel is correct. Most of their effort was spent planning and talking about what to do next. While you are executing military operations right under their nose, they play defense. You are executing positive military advantages, running offense, and moving the goalpost closer to unification."

I paused for a moment to gather my thoughts. "I have heard you lay out the complete planning for the unification of North and South Vietnam. As I listen to you speak about the mission of the North Vietnamese, I hear that Cambodia and Laos are in concert with the unification. I must add that half the population in South Vietnam is favorable, and they give support to the North. This leaves just a few Vietnamese in the South looking for a different government. Colonel, what a story to tell the world about, stating the real reasons for being involved with this conflict.

"You have mentioned oil. The first thing that comes to my mind is President Johnson and his friends' connections in Texas who are in the petroleum business. A French petroleum company has been in the South China Sea for years, pumping oil from shallow waters. President Kennedy wasn't interested in getting involved with this war in South Vietnam, and shortly into his presidential term he was assassinated in Dallas, Texas. Do you think that Vice President Johnson had anything to do with this assassination?"

"Jean Claude, you put me on the spot with this question," Colonel Gorky replied. "I don't have any intel on this subject. However, my opinion is very suspicious that the assassination happened in Vice President Johnson's home state of Texas. The trail of events that happened during the assassination is peculiar."

The colonel took a breath. "Jean Claude, we have been talking most of the night. Bopha has given me the high sign to come to bed. We can continue tomorrow if I have the time. Have I bored you enough for this evening by the river?"

"Colonel Gorky, I won't be able to sleep tonight thinking about all the territory, unification plans, and developments for Indochina's success," I replied. "I will be trying to put these major tasks into place. Maybe I can get my company to make a full-time place for me here. That would be a dream—having access to your office, sharing time with you and Bopha, and living close by with Angelina. This might have a chance of happening. I have talked too much and it's time to go to bed. Good night, Colonel. See you in the morning."

I was ready for a good day with Colonel Gorky. Part two would be interesting and I was itching to get my report back to Nha Trang. All the information I heard from the colonel was valuable, and it was important to return the drawings, photos, and the synopsis of the military attacks on three major cities in South Vietnam—Saigon, Nha Trang, and Khe Sanh. Time grew shorter each week. I had two months to collect the lunar new year attack plans.

The next morning, at breakfast, I greeted everyone. "Good morning, Bopha and Colonel Gorky. Good morning to you Lieutenant Colonel Pham, Major Tran, and Captain Duc. My, we have a full house this morning for breakfast. I am glad to be present with this fine lady and you gentlemen. I can't wait to dive into the Bopha breakfast menu. I have been waiting all night to see what Bopha would have for breakfast. Bopha, may I serve you breakfast?"

"Yes," Bopha replied, "I would enjoy having you serve me breakfast. This would be different, and I appreciate your kindness."

I turned and asked, "Colonel Gorky, may I serve you along with Bopha?"

"Jean Claude, are you looking for a position in the kitchen as a waiter?" Colonel Gorky asked.

I laughed. "Yes, I think I would enjoy this life. You have great friends and interesting contacts. I could be a waiter and journalist, based in the jungle of northeastern Cambodia. Well, I am serving Bopha and the colonel. May I serve you gentleman too?"

They replied yes, and then one asked me, "Jean Claude, will you do an article about this morning's breakfast?"

"I was thinking," I answered, "I would start in the kitchen with Bopha. Move around into the dining area for a group photo. However, I don't think group photos will be allowed."

Colonel Gorky nodded. "Jean Claude, you are right about the group photo. Only words can be used for your article if you wish to have a short story about Lieutenant Colonel Pham, Major Tran, and Capt. Duc. Your article will be printed in Hanoi newspapers only."

"I would be pleased to do a piece of short news about them," I said.

Colonel Gorky smiled. "Let's enjoy the breakfast out on the veranda this beautiful morning."

All of us helped move the food out on the veranda and sat down to eat. Bopha was happy to see us eat with a little discussion between us. I could see the relationship between the colonel and Bopha had developed into a steady love affair. I saw marriage might be in the cards.

I helped Bopha with some of the dishes, but the servers did most of the cleaning up. Bopha and I walked down to the river for a view of the riverboats. It was a pleasant visit and I enjoyed being around her. I told her I wanted to give her a letter for Angelina. The letter explained to Angelina what to do if anything happened to me in combat. Bopha was willing to give my letter to Angelina. I thanked her and stated that I trusted her and the colonel. I shared with Bopha that I would be leaving tomorrow morning on a mission to southern Cambodia.

"Bopha, I would love to speak with Angelina before I leave."

"I can arrange for you to phone right now," Bopha said.

"Oh, thank you, Bopha," I said.

Bopha called the palace and reached Angelina.

"Jean Claude, is this you?" Angelina asked.

"Yes, it's me," I replied. "I miss being around you and giving you warm hugs."

"Jean Claude," Angelina said, "come back to the palace! All of us here talk about you and how you made our home alive."

"I want to very much," I said. "Give my regards to your parents and the people at the palace. I will never forget them and all the enjoyment I had on my visit. For you, my love, I will try to see you again soon. I have been given assignments that will take me far away from the palace. When I return to Colonel Gorky's compound, I will call you."

"Jean Claude, you must come back to me," Angelina pleaded. "My life here has stopped, and I miss being with you! My mother thinks I am crazy over you. I tell her I am just like she was over my father."

I smiled. "You still have a good sense of humor."

We had a good cry over the phone. I don't remember too much of the conversation, but a lot of love was shared over the phone.

Finally, Angelina said, "Jean Claude, I must go now but my heart is crying out for your love."

"Angelina," I replied, "I will call you when I return to Colonel Gorky's compound. I love you."

CHAPTER 29

PART TWO

"Jean Claude, are you ready for part two of my lecture?" Colonel Gorky asked.

"Yes, sir, I am ready for your adventure and military plans," I replied.

"Jean Claude," Colonel Gorky began, "there are maps I want to show you in my office. I have been thinking about your proposal of writing news releases on the Tết attacks throughout South Vietnam. You are correct—there will be too much going on to capture all the action in South Vietnam during this time. My staff agrees with this plan of having other spies in Khe Sanh and Saigon. I am going to show you key maps of the three cities that will get hit the hardest. You already know my feelings about secrecy. If my planning is successful in these three cities, the war will be over. The major battle will be Khe Sanh. Khe Sanh is set in a valley, a gauntlet surrounded by mountains. It will be a long and hard battle. A lot of military people from both sides will die. If I come close to ending the conflict in Vietnam, I will move on to another position in Russia or maybe here in North Vietnam. I have been told my promotion to brigadier general is imminent. Don't tell anyone, but I will have a surprise party soon. You will be there and can write the article."

Colonel Gorky continued. "Jean Claude, I must tell you—there is a bounty on my head. You cannot take any photos of me. Drug lords wanted to stop the patrols from interrupting their business in Cambodia and Laos. They think killing me would stop them. They don't understand the complete picture of what is going on here in Southeast Asia."

"Does anyone else know?" I asked.

Colonel Gorky shook his head. "No, and let's keep it that way. I have strengthened my security and posted snipers on the perimeter of this compound. Also, patrols at night and day go out on scouting missions outside this compound. Just in case I do get killed, I am asking you to look out for Bopha. She respects you, and I trust you to keep her safe. Drug lords would likely cut her head off as well as mine, and use it as propaganda. This can't happen. I have left my last will and testament in the safe behind you, stating that you will have access to my assets to protect Bopha and provide funds for her lifestyle. It also states that you will have any military aid at your disposal. Please don't hesitate to use them. Go to Lieutenant Colonel Pham for your needs. Everything is set up and easy to understand. Lieutenant Colonel Pham, you can trust."

"Colonel, I will take these wishes of yours and perform them with my utmost abilities. I am honored to be of assistance to you and given this trust."

"Thank you," Colonel Gorky said. "But we have gone off track from part two. Let us get back and talk about Tết. Once again, my staff and I agree about writing articles before the attacks happen. All hell will break out on the first night of the lunar new year. What do you think about concentrating on the three major battles, Saigon, Nha Trang, and Ke Sanh?"

"How will I travel to these places and write articles about what is going to happen?" I asked. "The photograph reporting will be limited."

"I have made arrangements in Chiphu, Cambodia, and Tây Ninh City in South Vietnam for your new documents," Colonel Gorky said. "The new documents will show that your parents lived in Da Lat. Chiphu is a training center for our operations in the southern part of South Vietnam. All worthy French families had homes in Saigon and, during the hot season, would live in their villas on the lake in Da Lat.

The staff there will help you with clothing, disguise ideas, additional documents if needed, and give you a secret code to make contact in South Vietnam. We have spies all over South Vietnam, but especially in Saigon. They will contact you first. Lieutenant Colonel Pham will teach you how to disguise yourself and show you how to dress."

Colonel Gorky continued. "Now, these instructions are very important for you to remember: There is a restaurant in Saigon's largest Chinatown, Cholon, in District 13, that is owned and operated by a Viet Cong woman, Ms. Kim. Chiphu staff will give you her code to make contact. We use this location for most of the underground financial arrangements and communications. The American forces will not suspect you coming and going at this restaurant. Many foreign journalists have meals, or attend parties, with our—unknown to them—spies. Ladies who work there as waitresses are placed in this restaurant to get all the intel they can from the American GIs. With your new appearance, you will melt into the population just fine. You will be able to travel freely without any problems as a French photojournalist. But you must be very diligent and observant of your surroundings at all times. You are swimming with people who might want to harm you."

"Colonel Gorky, I have a lot of information to absorb and get organized."

"Jean Claude, I have more to share with you. I am going to outline future history with you right now. Are you ready?"

I nodded. "Yes, I will write it down, or will you give me this information on paper?"

"You better write it down and record this overall synopsis," Colonel Gorky replied. "You can use this information in your articles while in South Vietnam before Tết. What I am going to tell you will be happening during the Tết Offensive. Over one hundred thousand NVAs and

Viet Cong are ready to attack. Our goals are to weaken or destroy the South Vietnamese government and spark political instability in the South. Massive assaults will lead to defections and rebellions. Our six main objectives are in Saigon—specifically, Long Binh Headquarters, National Radio Station, Independence Palace, US Embassy, ARVN General Staff compound located near Tan Son Nhut Air Base, and Tan Son Nhut Air Base. The Viet Cong 9th Division will hit the 25th Infantry base at Củ Chi while the NVA will hit US 1st Infantry and ARVN 5th Division near Lai Ke. In Hue, Vietnam's ancient capital, Viet Cong and NVA troops will attack and take the walled fortress. In Nha Trang, at the First Field Force Victory Headquarters, Viet Cong will hide in concrete culverts near the soccer field. The sound of fireworks going off will conceal gunfire, giving a surprise to attacks. In Khe Sanh Combat Base, all hell is going to take place early on January 21, 1968. We have NVA and Viet Cong troops numbering up to forty thousand. They will rain on the US forces and ARVN troops, heavy mortar, rocket, and artillery bombardment, and small-scale ground attacks. I anticipate air strikes, B-52 carpet bombings, fighter bombers, and heavy artillery."

Colonel Gorky paused before he said, "Jean Claude, I want to tell you that some of our artillery cannons have been bored out. We have placed rifling inside the barrel to have a longer projectile range. The Tết Offensive must achieve a desire from the American people to stop supporting this war. We will show that we can fight outside the tunnels and into the streets. Jean Claude, I must honestly tell you that our military efforts might be a failure. However, the propaganda machine wins."

CHAPTER 30
NHA TRANG MAP

As we entered Colonel Gorky's office, I asked, "When will I leave for Chiphu? We are close to the South Vietnam border."

"Maybe in the morning. I must decide after I finish briefing you," Colonel Gorky answered.

"I need to have more information on Nha Trang that will receive a lot of attention during the Tết Offensive," I continued. "Is this the stack of maps on your conference table?"

"Yes," Colonel Gorky replied, "and on top is the map of Nha Trang. All the red dots are target buildings where high-ranking military personnel live. The Americans call these housing locations 'Macv compounds.' Other areas must be destroyed, like the Nha Trang Airport. Nha Trang is the military command center for the 5th Special Forces Group, Korean Rock Forces, US planning and strategy center, along with the CIA. This is the nest for operations in the second corp. All the dots are extremely important to destroy along with the occupants."

I had my secret body camera ready for this chance to take as many photos as possible. The chance I have been waiting for. The colonel moved away from the conference table but returned very quickly. I managed to take many photos of the Nha Trang map, glad the colonel hadn't seen any unusual movements from me.

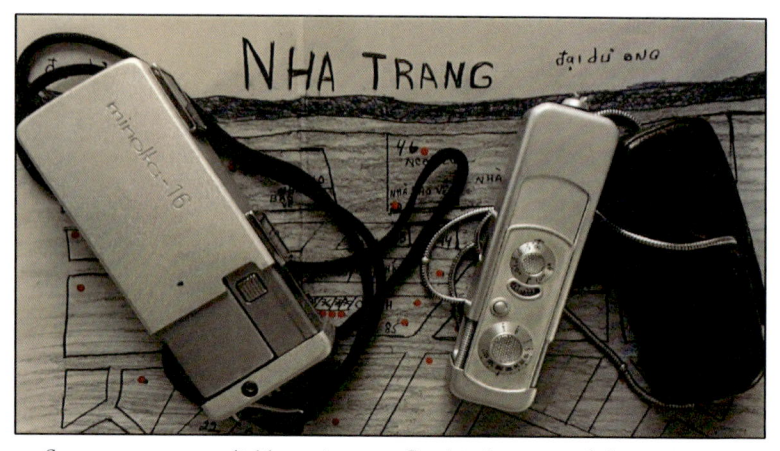

Spy cameras were reliable equipment. On this day, it saved American lives.

I believed I had captured enough intel to convince the people in Nha Trang that the Tết Offensive was real. When I arrived in Chiphu and prepared to enter South Vietnam, my contacts would be waiting for me in Tây Ninh or Củ Chi. I needed to be careful because I would be accompanied by Russian and North Vietnamese spies. Colonel Gorky wanted them to give me protection.

That night, I went over the steps about giving my handlers and assets intel—how to dress so they would notice me, how to place intel material at different locations, and how to notice them. But I had another layer of concern for my traveling companions: I couldn't be in a hurry to hand over the intel material. I needed to be careful not to expose myself, the handlers, and the assets in South Vietnam.

Author Jean Claude Martin in Nha Trang.
Photography by Sterling Stefferson

CHAPTER 31
CHIPHU, CAMBODIA

The next morning at breakfast with Bopha and Colonel Gorky, conversation around the table was light. I started by asking the colonel about my itinerary and what was in store for me today.

"You will be leaving for Chiphu by helicopter with Lieutenant Colonel Pham, Major Tran, and Captain Duc at eleven," Colonel Gorky began. "Bopha will contact Angelina. Jean Claude, you can't tell her where you are going. Nobody can know your assignment. Remember, I have arranged for bodyguards to accompany you throughout this mission. Newspaper coverage is important to the overall recording of this historical event. Nothing can happen to you. You are skilled with your understanding of the unification struggle going on here in Vietnam. Your coverage will be enormously valuable."

"Colonel," I said, "you fill my heart with colorful words. I will get the job done with the highest degree of success for your historical record. I feel honored to be in this position to be a force to bargain with. I need to return to Chiphu for transportation to Nha Trang for my assignment."

"You tell the person who is in charge what you want to do," Colonel Gorky replied. "They will lead the way to other destinations. This method will be used throughout your stay in South Vietnam."

I nodded, then rose from my chair. "Okay, I will get ready. Colonel, I sincerely appreciate your hospitality and for giving me protection while I am in South Vietnam. Thank you again."

In my room, I left a pack of things that I would need for this next assignment. Going through my things, I ran across photos I took with my regular camera of Angelina and me in Vientiane, Laos. The photos brought back fond memories of us; our experience together was the best of the best. Finally, I called Angelina to say "See you soon." It was a drama for both of us. We made it through the conversation and ended with the hope of seeing each other again soon.

I went to the helipad early, ready to start the trip to Chiphu and get going with the assignment. I also wanted to hand over the intel to my handler or asset as soon as I could. Time was working against me, however, and it was critical for the American soldiers to prepare for the attacks. The turning point in this war was at hand.

Landing at Chiphu, Cambodia, I was rushed off to a building for a quick introduction and received new documents, new clothing, disguise items, cameras, boots, and a backpack.

Then, Lieutenant Colonel Pham took me into his office and gave me instructions about what lay ahead. He was very informative with his program. I was assigned a room where I unpacked my things and looked over my new items. I got my things ready for tomorrow when I would head into Củ Chi for my first outing. I had a filling dinner, showered, and went to bed.

Around midnight, I was awoken by machine guns firing and helicopters flying overhead. I walked outside to see what was going on. A veteran NVA came and told me the action was in the Tây Ninh province area.

Machine guns firing traces and live rounds near the Tây Ninh and Cambodia border. Green tracers are the NVA and Viet Cong. Red tracers are the US forces and allies.

All of us returned to our rooms and tried to sleep. The night was full of activities in Tây Ninh.

Finally, morning came and everyone was stirring. I had slept with my clothes on just in case I had to go into combat. After our meal, we met in Lieutenant Colonel Pham's office for a short briefing.

Lieutenant Colonel Pham came up to me and said, "I didn't recognize you at first. You look completely different in your new outfit."

"I went to the supply room last night to pick out two sets of new fatigues," I replied. "Glad you like them. I had more choices here than Colonel Gorky's compound in Pak Nhai, Cambodia."

"I am glad to have you aboard here with us," Lieutenant Colonel Pham said. "Your humor is welcome."

"Will I be issued a weapon of my choice?" I asked Lieutenant Colonel Pham.

"What would you like?" Lieutenant Colonel Pham asked.

"Back in France, as a war correspondent," I said, "I had experience using a Beretta bobcat, in the calibers .25 or .32, with a silencer for some assignments."

"I will look into your request today," Lieutenant Colonel Pham said, "but I don't have any channels for foreign weapons. Would you settle for anything I can find with a silencer?"

I nodded. "Yes, and I appreciate your help."

Lieutenant Colonel Pham replied, "I will check and see if I can find this pistol and a silencer. I will have a better answer within a day or two. The Củ Chi tunnel complex can make you a silencer. We must find a handgun with a threaded barrel, or the Củ Chi armory can put it together for you."

After that, I met my two new companions, both of Vietnamese descent. Thankfully, Captain Duc could speak French, a great help. The other acted more like a come-along person. He didn't say very much, just waited to get instruction in Vietnamese from Captain Duc. We got our things loaded into an old US jeep and headed to the border of South Vietnam to head into Củ Chi. From Củ Chi, we would take different transportation into Saigon, District 13. There, we were introduced to the restaurant owner.

After meeting her on the sly, we had lunch and waited to meet another man of interest in Saigon's Chinatown, Cholon. After waiting most of the afternoon at the restaurant, a man who looked like Ho Chi Minh (the communist leader of the North Vietnam government) came in and sat down near our table. We began chatting about nothing of importance in the local language. We couldn't speak French inside the restaurant because this would bring attention to others at the restaurant.

We were directed to another place close to our safe house behind the restaurant. I needed to remember the address for future cover if needed.

Ms. Kim's handler at her restaurant in Cholon.

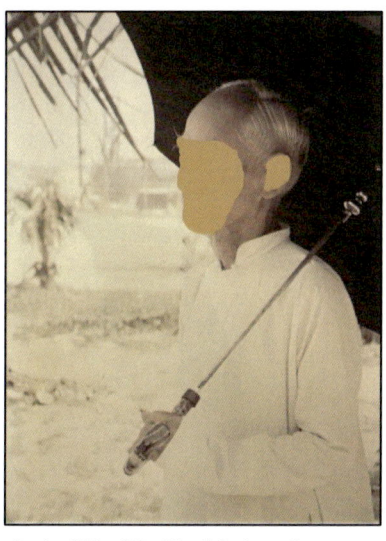

The asset who looked like Ho Chi Minh at the restaurant in Cholon.

CHAPTER 32
Củ Chi Tunnel Complex

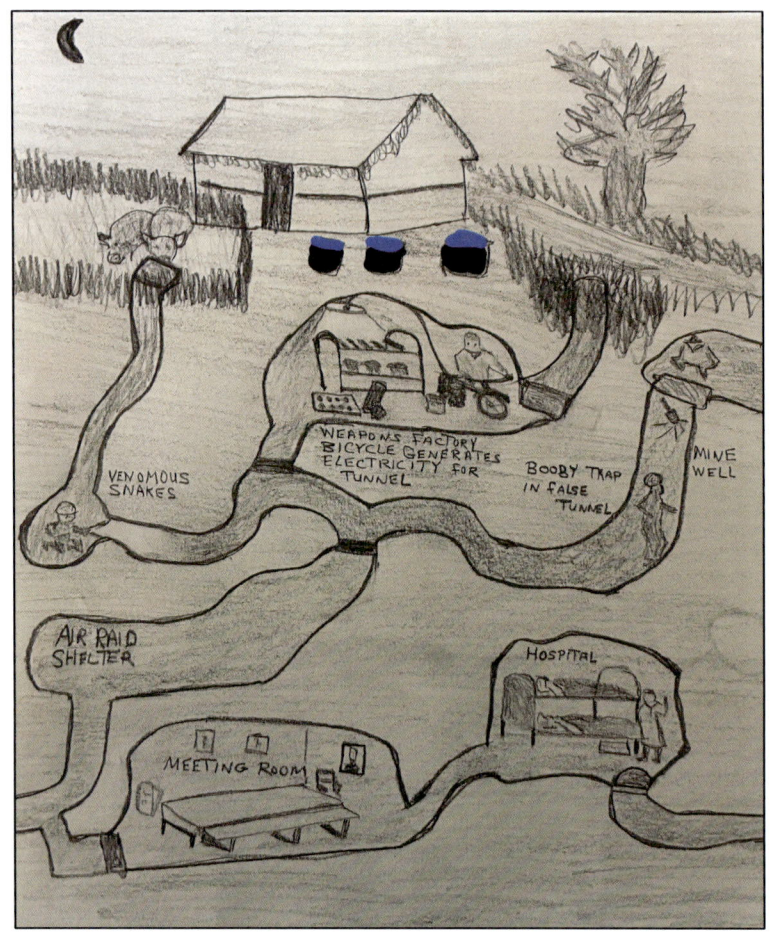

The Củ Chi tunnel (nicknamed Cong World) complex started in 1948 during French colonialism. It continued to improve over time. The Củ Chi tunnels were built on three levels—tunnels for soldiers, kitchens, booby trap areas, ventilated holes, and escape tunnels, all ending in a river. During the American war with North Vietnam, it expanded to 240 km (150 miles) of underground tunnels. The tunnel complex is 75 km (45 miles) from Saigon. Some tunnels were under the 25th Infantry Division. Ironically, the 25th Infantry was located on top of the Củ Chi tunnels. Later, in the 1960s, US carpet bombing finally destroyed most of the tunnel complex.

MY YEARS AS A WAR CORRESPONDENT

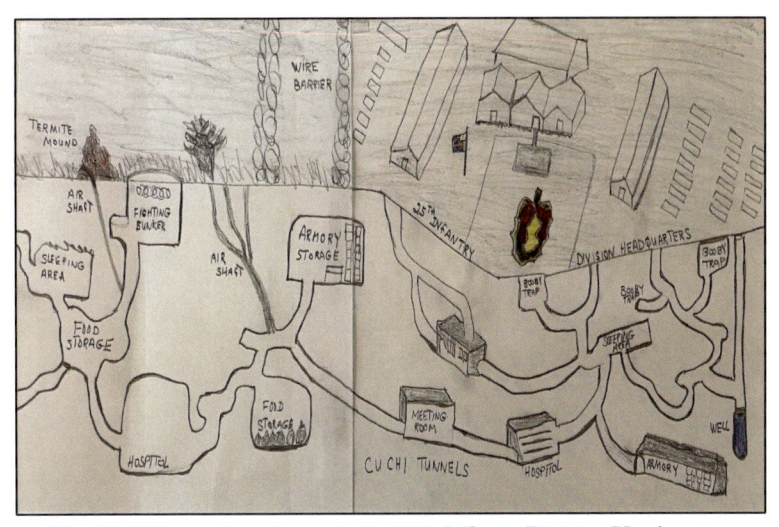

The Củ Chi tunnels underneath the 25th Infantry Division Headquarters.

Marked with red arrows are the entry and exit of the tunnels complex near Củ Chi. This Pigpen was used to disguise the tunnels.

This bamboo factory disguised as an underground tunnel complex. The escape tunnel opened to the river flowing on the other side of the fence. The red arrows show the underground tunnel path.

*Part of the Củ Chi bamboo factory disguise.
Red arrows show the underground tunnel path.*

CHAPTER 33
FINDING MY WAY

About one month before the lunar new year (Tết Offensive) was scheduled to happen, I was getting familiar with the high-target places. I needed to know the names of streets and buildings, meet my handlers and assets in these key cities. Basically, know the lay of the land and who the players were.

I was staying in Saigon for a few days and going to Nha Trang to prerecord target places. Once the Tết Offensive began, I would get all the important photos and write what I saw in Nha Trang while Khe Sanh would be the main battlefield.

Something else I needed to be knowledgeable about was the travel patterns, specifically how arrangements would be made to travel during the large-scale battle chaos. This country would be torn apart. I might have restrictions on traveling during the Tết Offensive days and weeks. I needed to make

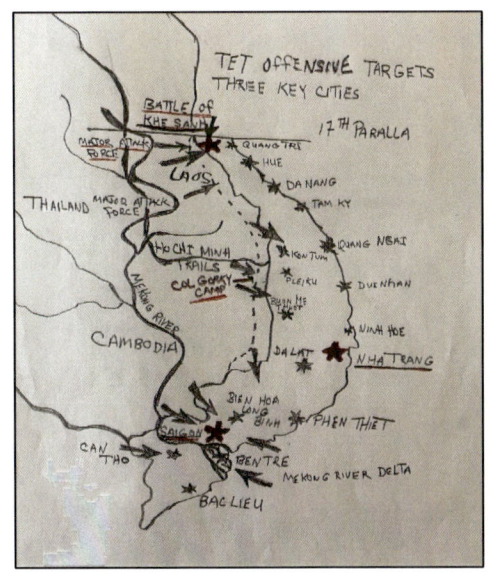

Colonel Gorky's camp and major cities in South Vietnam during the Tết Offensive. The Khe Sanh battle was planned to be the final American battle in South Vietnam.

plans to move around these restrictions if they were placed on journalists. I believed that Colonel Gorky's spies would not be allowed to board aircraft during this chaotic period. This would be great for me; I'd be alone, able to move around freely, feeding intel to Nha Trang.

The Têt Offensive would be a history-maker—the shot heard around the world.

I closed my eyes and dreamed about being in Vermont with Sofie. I wondered what Sofie might be doing now and if she was wondering why she hadn't heard a word from me. Sofie seemed so far from me. I couldn't remember all the exciting times I shared with her and my friends.

When I looked in the mirror, I saw a young man who had grown into a man.

Captain Duc had looked content coming out of the meeting. He had a meeting with a handler. Ms. Kim received new orders—we were going back to Chiphu.

On the way, I was uncomfortable being in this area. There was too much happening all around us—US convoys, US ground troop movements, and the Viet Cong taking notice of their activities. I expected guns to fire at any moment.

We made it back to the Chiphu compound just in time for chow. I looked around the table and saw happy faces. Earlier, these faces looked a little scared. It felt good to be back in the compound.

Lieutenant Colonel Pham came out and asked if I could come to his office once I finished with my meal.

"Yes, I can," I told him, "and if it is urgent, I will come with you now."

"No, I have your request in my office," Lieutenant Colonel Pham replied.

"Oh, I will come right now! I want to see and handle my surprise."

"Okay, come on," Lieutenant Colonel Pham said.

"Where did you find the .25 Beretta and silencer?" I asked.

"I had a friend who had this pistol with a silencer," Lieutenant Colonel Pham explained. He then turned to me and asked, "You saw combat in Laos?"

"Yes, sir," I replied, "I was taking a shower at a nearby waterfall. While walking back to the campsite, the jungle came alive with gunfire and RPGs. We were engaged in hand-to-hand fighting as well."

"Yes, Colonel Gorky has told me about your two encounters," Lieutenant Colonel Pham said. "Some of Colonel Gorky's staff have high regard for you. Jean Claude, I must tell you I have been promoted to colonel today."

"Congratulations! I am happy for you and your family. Do you know if Colonel Gorky got promoted too?"

"I do not. If he has been, I will let you know," he replied.

I nodded my head and said, "Please, when you do speak with him, give him my regards. I'm looking forward to seeing him after Tết is over."

Colonel Pham continued. "I have plans for you. Tomorrow morning, you will be going to Saigon with Captain Duc. Both of you will board a US military aircraft for Nha Trang. I am concerned about traveling from one city to another during the offensive. South Vietnam will be in chaos for the first few days. You need to get to Nha Trang to report on the battles. In the morning, the three of us will meet in my office and go over the strategy."

"Okay," I said. "Colonel Pham, if that is all you have for me, I would like to finish my meal, take a shower, and clean the Beretta before going to bed. When I return here from the Tết Offensive mission, I will return the weapon to you. Tomorrow will be a busy day for all of us."

Colonel Pham nodded. "Good night, Jean Claude. Thanks for thinking about the Berretta. My friend will be pleased to have it back."

Morning came early and I was on my way to Saigon with Captain Duc. Both of us had our press IDs, and we would see if we could get on a flight to Nha Trang. In one regard, I felt comfortable with Captain Duc. Maybe he could speak French with me. I needed to remind him not to speak too much Vietnamese around the airport personnel. They might not let him on the flight if he was speaking Vietnamese.

Beretta Bobcat 25 Auto with a silencer.

CHAPTER 34
NHA TRANG

We stopped off at the restaurant in District 13 for some money and to get additional documents. Captain Duc took care of these tasks. I waited outside at the restaurant near the busy street. When Captain Duc returned, we traveled to the Tan Son Nhat Airport. It was heavily guarded. This would be a dry run to see if we could get on the flight. At the check-in counter, they separated us, but I didn't have any problems getting on the flight to Nha Tang. However, Captain Duc would not be joining me. They refused him passage and turned him away from the airport, MPs escorting him to the street.

They asked me a few questions about Captain Duc, and I simply told them he is working for a foreign news outlet. We met at the Rex Hotel and had breakfast together, then shared a taxi to the airport. They accepted my response and let me board the flight to Nha Trang.

I was very relieved to have the chance to operate alone. I planned to check into the intel center with a handler in Nha Trang and tell them about the Tết Offensive. I needed to keep my eyes open for Colonel Gorky's and Colonel Pham's spies. They would be alerted in Nha Trang, and were waiting for my arrival at the Nha Trang Airport.

Once I got there, I would be looking for a cyclo taxi. It could be friendly or foe. After the plane landed at the airport, military people were scurrying around. They didn't notice me— I was just another news report. I didn't see any Russian or Vietnamese spies at the baggage claim area. However, I did see one of my assets.

I didn't approach the asset right away. I was distant, watching in all directions for any person who looked suspicious. Finally, I gave my asset a code to which he offered his cyclo. I still was very distant from him. Spies could be anywhere watching the airport. The cyclo driver took me to a safe house location in Nha Trang.

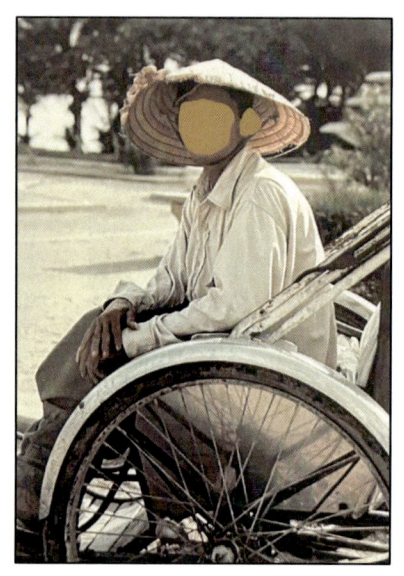

Mr. Chi, a cyclo asset in Nha Trang, South Vietnam.

The cyclo driver, Mr. Chi, began giving orders to me in French. "Walk down the street to a villa on the left side painted light blue and faded yellow. You will be met by two people, a Vietnamese lady and man. It looks from the outside like a whore house, but it's your safe house for the time being. They will arrange for other cyclo drivers to take you around Nha Trang. The intel group is very anxious to have a briefing with you right away. Plans are set for this evening in a location we don't know yet. Someone will come for you early this evening and pick you up. Stay in your room and wait for the contact to come for you."

"How will I know the pickup contact is real?" I asked.

"You must exchange codes," Mr. Chi replied. "Dress in your contact ID clothing, the same protocol you have been using. I know who you are. You have made history with the intel staff here at Nha Trang headquarters."

"I hope the history is positive."

"You will see once you have your briefing this evening."

"I feel strange being around people who are on my side of the war," I said. "For months, I have been in the enemy's hands, all the while watching out for danger. When I go to bed, I make the bed look like someone is sleeping in it, I sit in a dark corner chair watching the windows and doors or in the next room listening for any unwanted noise. I put alarms around the windows and doors. Just in case I didn't wake up right away. Do you know if Lieutenant Colonel Steve Miller is still the head intelligence officer?"

I don't know about the inner circle people," Mr. Chi replied. "I just take people like yourself around Nha Trang and point out the safe places you can go to. The handler will pick you up this evening."

I nodded. "Thanks for your help and have a safe day."

Once inside the safe house, I went to my room at the top of the stairs and down the hall. The room was spacious and comfortable. I still couldn't let my guard down.

After taking a shower, I lay down for a while on the bed. I didn't sleep, just rested. I then went downstairs to see if I could get a cold water and a bit to eat. Nobody was in the makeshift kitchen. I looked around for something to eat. I was able to find water to drink but no food. I went back upstairs and looked out the window, where the street below was busy with people walking by. I returned to bed for a rest.

Time went by slowly when you were waiting to receive a message. Finally, I got word that someone was in the lobby asking for me. I slowly got dressed and took my pistol and a small knife with me. I was dressed in a woman's brown wig under a baseball cap, false glasses, old pants, a shirt, and funny-looking shoes. When I arrived in the lobby, I looked around until I saw a person standing next to the bar.

He asked me for a code, but I was reluctant to speak. I walked over to the office door and noticed something strange about his shoes, for my handler's shoes told me differently. I ignored him and walked through the office door and into another room that led to the outside. I continued to have doubts about the person who followed me.

I took a small side street going toward a dark alley. He continued following me, getting closer, until I stopped and confronted him. I forced him into the wall, driving my pistol into his chest—but *he* turned out to be a *she*. I could tell by the size of this person's breasts, that she was a female. This explained why the shoes looked different. A man wouldn't be wearing that style of shoes in this situation.

I put my Beretta away and gave her a code. She didn't answer me correctly and I quickly brought the Beretta back out and pointed it at her heart.

I began to ask her questions about who she was and what she was doing here waiting for me.

She spoke in Vietnamese. "There is a bounty on your head. You killed the son of a Cambodian drug lord, and he wants you captured and brought to him. We are here to disable you and transport you back to Cambodia."

"Who is 'we'?" I replied in Vietnamese.

"Look behind you!" she shouted back.

I turned to find three men standing with primitive weapons, the type from the jungle regions. I immediately, and without hesitation, went into action defending myself. I shot the woman I still had against the wall and turned to address the others. Two of the men swung their sickles, and I shot one in the leg and the other one in the arm with the sickle. The third wanted to use his skills in martial arts, but he was quickly outmatched. I shot the first two in their heads, angling the barrel of my gun upward. The small caliber bullet would rattle around in their skulls, tearing up their brains. I shot the martial arts expert twice in the head.

I had to find Mr. Chi and get a cleaner to remove the bodies from this scene. I returned to the street in front of the whore house and looked in both directions. At first, I didn't see Mr. Chi, but soon, I saw him in the distance sitting in his cyclo. He spotted me and came over very slowly. I asked him to take me for a ride around the block.

During the trip, I told him what happened and that I needed a cleaner to come and remove the bodies from the alley. My disguise was torn and I needed to get off the street. I asked him to take me back to the whore house. I took the outside stairs to my room. Meanwhile, the cleaners came and removed the four mystery people.

I needed to find out more about this drug lord from Cambodia. How did they know who I was and where I would be staying? I needed to tighten up my security. I gathered all my things and quietly left the whore house and went across the street to another whore house. I got a room facing the house I just came from. I wanted to see who might enter and what messages might be sent to me. I asked Mr. Chi if someone would be coming to pick me up this evening. I also asked him to keep me informed and told him I would be on the lookout for suspicious people too.

"At seven o'clock," Mr. Chi told me late in French, "there will be an old black sedan in front of this building to pick you up. Dress normally and bring all the intel to date with you. You will meet Colonel Black. He has just taken over Lieutenant Colonel Miller's position. They are very interested in seeing and discussing your journey. Reports have stated that you were shot in the leg and killed three or more adversaries and that you have a relationship with the future president of Laos's daughter. To top it off, your relationship with a KBG high-ranking officer in Cambodia is also spreading. They want to know what else about your encounters they don't know."

CHAPTER 35
INTERROGATION ON A US NAVY SHIP

Time moved slowly while I waited to be picked up. But sure enough, two men came into the lobby. I was standing in the corner next to the exit door. The man who seemed to be in charge put a see-through burlap bag over my head. They rushed me into their vehicle, and off I went to a helipad.

I flew to an offshore ship, and when we landed, I was taken to a twenty-foot-long container that had been converted into an irrigation room. I felt like a POW. I looked around the container and saw the following items on display: a storyboard with my photos and small pieces of note paper, musical speakers, motion-picture cameras, microphones, special lighting, waterboarding devices, handcuffs, leg shackles, and other unwanted equipment I had only seen in movies. I had a sinking feeling come over me. I was sick to my stomach. What was going to happen to me? I was just doing my job, yet here I was out to sea and confined in a twenty-foot-long container.

Finally, men in uniform came into the container, and everyone in the container stood up, but I was a French journalist and citizen of France. Legally they didn't have any jurisdiction in holding me in confinement.

Everyone took their position and the man I assumed to be Colonel Black asked, in English, "Jean Claude, did you leave bodies at each safe house on your journeys?"

"Yes," I replied in French. "If I have to defend myself, I will use deadly force."

"Please respond to our questions in English," Colonel Black said. He then looked back at the booklet in front of him and started asking questions again. "What is your name, MOS, rank, and service number?"

"Name: Jean Claude Martin," I replied in French. "MOS: not applicable. Rank: not applicable. Service number: not applicable."

Colonel Black sighed. "You must answer these questions in English. Tell us about Hanoi."

I responded in broken English. "Sent by *La Combat-Haute-Savoie* newspaper. I report back to the newspaper for printing articles and return intel to my handlers and assets while in the field. In general, reporting anything that had intelligence value. Give to my handlers and assets along my journey from Hanoi, Laos, Cambodia, and South Vietnam." I continued, "You have board in here. It tells about my adventure. Why am I brought here? I was expecting a filet steak dinner with French wine."

Colonel Black ignored my questions. "Tell us about Laos."

"I travel down the Ho Chi Minh trail networks," I said. "Take photos and write intel notes of the areas I see. Gave this intel to handlers or assets along my journey to Pak Nhai, Cambodia. East of Nhong, Laos, in the remote jungle, had my first hand-to-hand combat experience. Had another combat experience east of Andoung Meas, Cambodia. Shot in the thigh with a small caliber pistol by drug mercenaries. Went to a compound outside Pak Nhai, Cambodia. The doctor helped the wound and I met Colonel Gorky."

"Tell us about Cambodia," Colonel Black ordered.

"I stayed with Colonel Gorky and was invited to go to Vientiane, Laos, by the Prince of Laos to visit his daughter, Angelina, who I met at the banquet in Hanoi. Angelina was at Colonel Gorky's villa. Colonel Gorky is an ally of the Laos government and does business with her father. At the palace, I saw a pile of maps, and Nha Trang was on top. I couldn't take pictures. CCTV cameras were everywhere. I had to find another way to get this intel to Nha Trang. Sometime later in my stay with Colonel Gorky, I had my chance. You have these photos and reports. I can see most of the intel here on the storyboard. All this intel on the storyboard I have given to my handlers and assets.

"The first evening of Tết is the beginning of a hell-breaking battle in South Vietnam. Tết will be remembered in the history books as the first time the NVA came out of the tunnels and fought the Americans with massive strength. For those people who don't think this intel is real, go to Khe Sanh and pick out a front-row seat. Colonel Gorky, the military architect of the Vietnam War and NVA command, believes this battle in Khe Sanh Valley will be the longest-fought battle in the Tết Offensive. With all due respect, *protect the men and women who will be on the front lines in Saigon, Nha Trang, and Khe Sanh*! I think all encampments in South Vietnam will be hit, some harder than others. Please do everything you can to get prepared for these attacks throughout South Vietnam. This is *real*, gentlemen."

Colonel Black didn't react. "Tell us about South Vietnam."

I went on. "Before I was sent to South Vietnam from Cambodia, my mission was Nha Trang. Document the areas around Nha Trang that would be hit during the Tết Offensive. I must write articles about the Nha Trang areas before and after the attacks. I will be able to cover more places while the fighting is going on. I will take more photos and write articles about Nha Trang before returning to Cambodia. On the eve of the lunar new year, I will be in Nha Trang covering the night action. Colonel Gorky will have his agents in Khe Sanh and Saigon covering their offensive. I need travel passes to travel freely around Nha Trang."

"Why should I allow you to have this privilege?" Colonel Black asked.

"Colonel Gorky, along with the 559th Engineer Corps," I replied, "has improved the supply network in South Vietnam over the years. The total organization of the NVA and Viet Cong are controlling two neighboring countries. I have provided top-secret military plans and distribution on how the farms in South Vietnam are operated. You need me to continue my relationship with Colonel Gorky and his team. I have given you this intel on a golden platter. You can save thousands of lives on both sides. Colonel Gorky expects me to photograph and write articles about the Tết Offensive, whether it is favorable or not to his side. I need to be able to travel and record all the actions and report back to Colonel Gorky once the battles have slowed down or finished. I must travel back to his headquarters in Cambodia."

I continued. "Colonel Black, it is up to you and all the American generals in Vietnam to get ready for these attacks. After I report back to Colonel Gorky, I don't know what is going to happen to me. This whole Tết build-up could blow up in Colonel Gorky's face. You gentlemen in this room can make this happen."

I then turned to another person and said, "The person sitting in the corner, who are you and what is your name?"

"I am with the Central Intelligence Agency," the man in the corner replied.

"Okay," I said, "do you have a name? I have heard numerous times that the NVA and Viet Cong teach their mules, and Viet Cong farmers, for the parties you give them when captured, to feed you bogus intel about their operations. Your operations here in Vietnam entertain Colonel Gorky. Do you have a dossier on him? Can I have your name?"

"Your security clearance isn't high enough for me to tell you," he replied.

"Fine, what are you doing about protecting the secret outpost at Phou Pha Thi Mountain in Laos called 'Lima Site 85'?"

"I am not aware of such a site in Laos," he said.

I smiled. "Lima Site 85 has been hidden from the US public. Sir, this is a very important intel I am going to give you. I don't know what level of security clearance you have, but Lima Site 85 will be overrun this year. The Tactical Air Navigation System used by military aircraft equipment will be used against our forces. Command from the North Vietnamese special forces has been training to scale the cliff and take control of this site. The CIA has personnel along with several US Air Force personnel totaling around twenty."

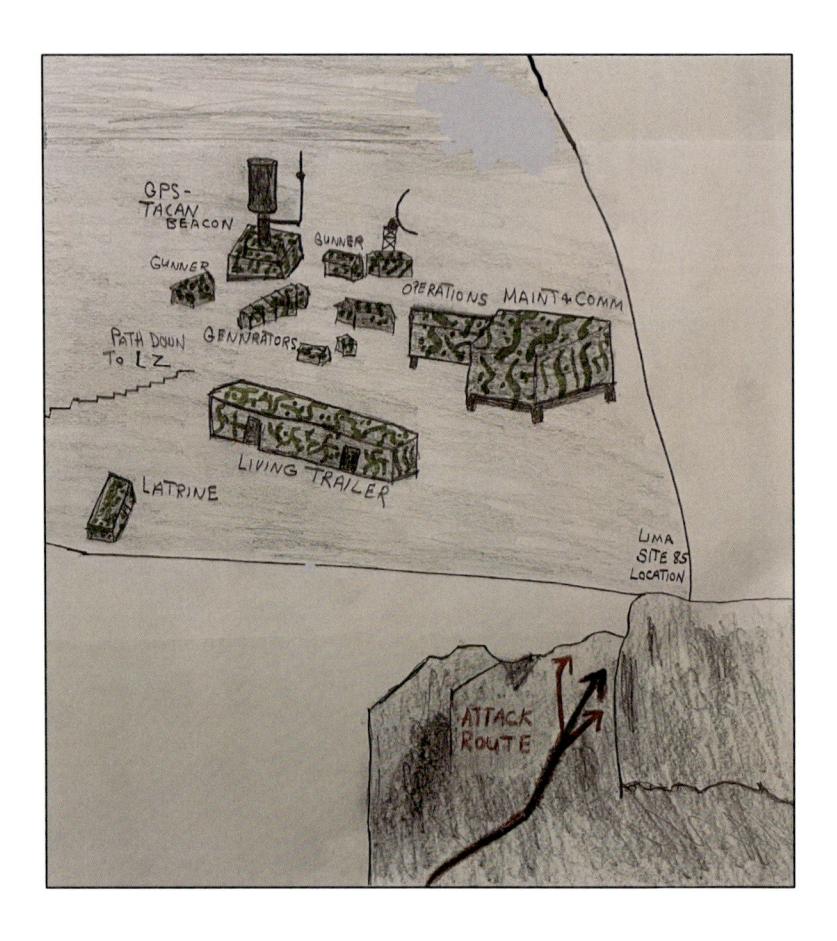

[Hand-drawn map of Lima Site 85 showing: GPS-TACAN Beacon, Gunner positions, Operations, Maint & Comm building, Generators, Path Down to LZ, Living Trailer, Latrine, Lima Site 85 Location, and Attack Route up the cliff]

"Why should I believe you?"

"Once you witness the Tết Offensive bloodshed on both sides," I replied, "you will be informed by your office staff that all forces in South Vietnam weren't prepared for these actions throughout the country. You will be responsible for thousands of dead and wounded civilians. I will add that you *do* know about Lima Site 85. There are other Lima sites in Laos but Lima Site 85 is the most important location. It is about one hundred and thirty miles west of Hanoi."

The CIA man scoffed. "I am leaving this silly meeting. I have more important matters to attend to."

"Okay," Colonel Black interjected, "I have heard enough for one night. Let us call this meeting finished. Have a good rest gentleman, and Jean Claude, you will stay. We must get you back over to Nha Trang very shortly, or you might be missed by the Russian spy network and local spies."

I nodded. "Yes, sir."

"Jean Claude," Colonel Black said, "you can speak to me in French. I want to know more about Colonel Gorky and get into more detail about the Tết Offensive with you right now. Show me the map of Nha Trang and tell me what you know might happen. How did you get to build trust with Colonel Gorky? I am interested in hearing more from you about your adventures. You must be tired of this."

I nodded. "Yes, sir, I am tired from all the drama today. However, I want to help you protect our servicemen and women. Oh, and thank you for turning around your line of questioning. Most of those attending the meeting had a better handle on what message I had for them. I am hoping this group of intel planners will use their resources to save lives. I appreciate your understanding of what I was going through every day in Laos and Cambodia."

I then went over, step by step, my relationship with Colonel Gorky and told Colonel Black that my stay overall was very important to the Vietnam War cause. I had the privilege to see some of the tunneling, how the suppliers were moved from one location to another, and how they used false trails to lure the US air strikes. I also explained how the mules were organized. This cycle was one of the supply networks that was very successful. I described how the people who carry out these missions were trained to give false information to the CIA if captured and showed my drawing to Colonel Black, which displayed how a web of people worked to make this strategy work toward the unification goal of North and South Vietnam.

My explanation of the Tết Offensive was lengthy and I had information he had never heard about as well as the plans for before Tết, during, and after the lunar new year celebration was over.

Colonel Black finally spoke. "Jean Claude, what are we going to do with you? It is time for you to return to the States. Are you anxious to leave Vietnam?"

I shook my head. "No, I must finish my mission with Colonel Gorky. I have penetrated the high command of the Russian, Laotian, Cambodian, and North Vietnamese military establishments and made acquaintances with his staff. I want to continue to gather intel from him. I feel comfortable being around Colonel Gorky, listening and witnessing what might happen, and delivering this intel to my handlers. I need to be part of this team to protect our troops in South Vietnam. I would enjoy a vacation from Vietnam.

"My exit from Colonel Gorky could be the following scenario: If he is successful with the Tết Offensive, Colonel Gorky will be promoted to Brigadier General Gorky and will go back to Moscow. If the Tết Offensive is a failure, Colonel Gorky will go back to Moscow. Colonel Pham would then replace Colonel Gorky if he is successful or not. Colonel Pham knows and trusts me. My whole relationship is important to carry forward into the future for the US campaign in Vietnam. I enjoy this type of work, and I am good at the job. My exit from this region must be real and sincere. I can use the trust which has been built on my first tour of duty to remain genuine."

I paused to let my request sink in, then continued. "I know Colonel Gorky. He could join me, along with the princess from Cambodia and

Angelina from Laos on my trip back to France. The chalet in Chamonix has many pictures of me on the walls. It is perfect and I would enjoy having their company in Chamonix. I still have friends that know I am working for a French newspaper in Vietnam. We could go to the newspaper and see some of my articles and photos. Colonel Gorky would eat this up. If I can't return to Vietnam, it would be a blow to your intel network.

"When I return to the States, I would like to be stationed on the west coast. My sister and her husband live in Sunnyvale, California, and I was thinking of Fort Ord and being assigned to the Combat Experimentation Command. I would report Mondays at noon and leave Fridays at noon. I could even live in officers' quarters at Fort Ord and wear suitable civilian clothing."

Colonel Black looked at me with wide eyes. "Wow, Jean Claude, you have left me speechless. I will have to go over all these possibilities that you have stated. I have been in this position for many years, and you are the first to have this drive to protect, willing to live in a dangerous environment and serve at the same time. I want to hear more about Lima Site 85. What you know and how you know this information. The man with the CIA is William Coleman, the deputy director of this region. He only answers to the director of the CIA. I don't think he appreciated your attitude. He relishes respect from people who take orders from him. He usually dominates meetings, but your meeting with us took the thunder away from him."

"I was focused on your team and answered questions accordingly. Can we talk about me returning to Vietnam?"

"Jean Claude, I must discuss this with my staff and superior officers," Colonel Black replied. "This is an unusual request and situation. I don't know if everyone will agree to have you return. You have put yourself in a strong position with all your high-level intelligence gathering.

Nobody—and I mean *nobody*—has been in your situation before. Now, off the record, I would have you back here continuing your work with Colonel Gorky or Lieutenant Colonel Pham right after your leave. You have been with the other side for over ten months without rest and recuperation leave. You are required to have two weeks while servicing in Vietnam. But I will recommend you return to duty with Colonel Gorky and come back through Hanoi and travel with the NVA and Viet Cong."

"If I can return to Vietnam," I said, "I must leave through Thailand. Colonel Gorky will get me there. I'll travel to France and return to Hanoi from there, just like my first trip to North Vietnam."

"You are a seasoned spy, Jean Claude," Colonel Black said. "You have gathered intelligence that is very valuable and extremely useful. All this evidence brought forward by you will only help your argument for returning to Vietnam."

"Is Colonel Winter still in his position in France?" I asked.

"Yes, he has retired from the military but taken a position as a civilian doing the same training."

"If Colonel Gorky and his party come with me to Chamonix, I would enjoy meeting with Colonel Winter before returning to Hanoi."

"Jean Claude, if you are coming back to Vietnam," Colonel Black said, "I can eliminate most of your airplane travel. To protect your standing with Colonel Gorky. I am going to request in my recommendations that you have sixty days' leave, which is a must-have after serving over a year in a combat zone. This should give you time to visit friends and be with your family members. Once you have completed your leave time, I suggest two days before flying to Geneva and entering Thonon-les-Bains, France. I will arrange for Colonel Winter's office staff to meet you just like the first time."

"Will I be issued a US passport before leaving for Boston?" I asked.

Colonel Black nodded. "I will have your US passport ready for you at Colonel Winter's office in Geneva. I will give you his information. His staff will be on notice for your arrival. Now, I know it is late in the evening, but I want to hear about Lima Site 85 and any information from you before going back to Nha Trang tonight."

CHAPTER 36
LIMA SITE 85, NORTHEAST LAOS

"I don't know too much about this site," I began, "but the following I do know from Colonel Gorky's meetings and general talk around the kitchen table. I will outline what I saw and heard. I have a drawing of the site I can show you. I wished Agent Coleman would have taken this meeting a little more seriously, but he knows more about this site than I probably do. The location is Phou Pha Thi Mountain, about 130 miles west of Hanoi. There were CIA and Air Force personnel—about twenty in all—and some type of TACAN radar navigation system at this site. The base is on top of a cliff, about six thousand feet high. You can't walk to this outpost so it has a short air landing strip. Colonel Gorky has commandos training to attack this outpost, and they will attack sometime after the Tết Offensive."[3]

I took a breath. "Colonel Black, I don't know anything else about Lima Site 85. Colonel Gorky has said that other outposts like this one are in Laos. But Lima Site 85 is the highest priority."

---

[3] *In the summer of 1966, about 130 miles west of Hanoi, the US Air Force and CIA put operational radar navigation equipment on top of a cliff of Phou Pha Thi Mountain, about six thousand feet high, in Laos, known as Lima Site 85. On March 12, 1968, an elite force of thirty men from the North Vietnamese Army overran the site and took control. US personnel were killed and a few were captured.*

"This is exciting intel. You have given me extraordinary information," Colonel Black replied. "What Agent Coleman will do about this intel is another story."

"Colonel Gorky and his staff, in general, don't think too highly of our intelligence gathering," I continued. "The CIA is fighting a war in Laos recruiting local Hmong. These ethnic minority mercenaries use guerilla warfare against the communists of Laos who support North Vietnam. I would like to return to Nha Trang and complete my mission for Colonel Gorky. By now, I'm sure his spies in Nha Trang are wondering where I am. I have been gone for a while. My personal items are in my locker at headquarters. Could you have someone break the lock and mail them to my parents? The clothing was put in the trash. I would appreciate this because I won't be returning to that room. Someone else could use the space."

"Let's get something to eat," Colonel Black said. "After the meal, we'll take you back to a different safe house in Nha Trang and you can continue with your mission. From there you are on your own. Be very careful, Jean Claude, there are spies from the other side all over this country. I will take care of your personal items and complete your request for leave and new assignment tomorrow morning to give to Brigadier General Palmer here in Nha Trang to approve. Good luck!"

I returned to the safe house and went upstairs to my bedroom. I took a shower, got dressed, and was ready to go out and see what was worth recording. I covered most of Nha Trang's high-target areas and moved around with Mr. Chi. He paddled me around the city. I didn't let him know I was taking photos along the way. I returned to the safe house where Mr. Chi gave me a message. The instructions were for me to go upstairs to my room and check inside my thirty-five-millimeter camera. The message inside stated that Mr. Chi would come in the morning to pick me up at the next corner for a tour of Nha Trang.

CHAPTER 37
KHE SANH VALLEY

Mr. Chi came to pick me up about ten minutes after seven. He carried an urgent letter for me from Colonel Gorky. The handler in Nha Trang, Mr. Dinh, had given it to Mr. Chi and ordered him to give it to me in a closed area. Mr. Chi and I went to a men's restroom down an alley.

The letter from Colonel Gorky stated the artillery blitzkrieg on Khe Sanh would hit everything of importance and blow up the main ammunition and ordinates that supported the forces in Khe Sanh on January 21, 1968. What a surprise for the world to see on television. For the most part, the US forces didn't have time to prepare for this attack. The upcoming attacks throughout South Vietnam would happen mainly on January 31, 1968. In Khe Sanh, it would start on January 21.

Colonel Gorky wanted to put the US Forces' eyes on Khe Sanh while the NVA and Viet Cong would be gearing up to hit all the major cities and villages in South Vietnam at 03:00 on January 31, 1968. Most of the South Vietnamese Army (ARVN) would be on leave for Tết. This meant that there would only be minimal forces on duty in Saigon, Nha Trang, and Hue.

Displaced people from the Nha Trang Tết Offensive battle.
In Khe Sanh, 205 Marines died, and 1,600 were wounded over the seventy-seven-day battle. The North Vietnamese Army and Viet Cong had 12,000 to 20,000 killed and 14,000 to 18,000 wounded. There were displaced men, women, and children of an estimated 1.7 million persons in South Vietnam. Civilians killed during the war numbered 8,000 and 19,000 were wounded. Seventy-six thousand homes were destroyed and seven hundred thousand people became refugees.

CHAPTER 38
BATTLE OF NHA TRANG

I was late getting into Nha Trang for the Tết Offensive battles. Nha Trang was exploding with combat areas all over. Military Assistance Command Vietnam (MACV) compounds were being hit with guerilla forces. Private villas were being attacked. Small arms firing sounded rapidly in every street. It was difficult for me to get around, but I was expecting this and had Mr. Chi nearby with his cyclo. I could use him to move me around to get photos and make notes of the attacks.

The heavy firing of small arms in and around Nha Trang made my air coverage a little touch and go. I finally arrived at the airport in a remote area that was safe for the time being.

Airplane view of the largest Buddha in Nha Trang, South Vietnam.

US soldiers were ready for attacks from the Viet Cong in Nha Trang.

US soldiers on rooftops looked for targets on the ground in Nha Trang.

US soldiers on watch for VC targets in Nha Trang during the Tết Offensive.

I managed to get into the action shortly after reaching the edge of town near the 5th Special Forces Group encampment behind the airport. I ran from place to place, asking where exceptional photo coverage might be and where the action was in town. I could see catastrophe everywhere

I looked—school buildings, government buildings, villas, homes, and airports. MACV troop installations encampments throughout Nha Trang were under attack.

*North Vietnamese Army and Viet Cong
were hauled up in these buildings in Nha Trang.*

A MACV compound hit by Viet Cong in Nha Trang.

Viet Cong hid in cement culverts near athletic fields in Nha Trang, waiting for the command to attack.

While I fought my way out of Nha Trang, on the way to Saigon, I witnessed the horrible sights of destruction, displaced people, families separated, and smoking buildings that had been hit by fighter aircraft with air-to-surface missiles. US helicopters flew close to the ground, shooting missiles at targets, usually Viet Cong holdouts in old farm villages. My ride on the back of a motorcycle was dangerous and I didn't know who was waiting for me along the road.

The trip to Saigon on the map looked short, but on the motorcycle, it was a difficult and long ride. Mr. Long, the Vietnamese man who was giving me a ride, had trails and bypasses that we took. From time to time, I thought he was taking me to my death. I had to rely upon my faith and trust in God to protect me.

We cut back and forth on different roads and trails to get into the northern sector of Saigon, known as Bien Hoa. From there, I took another motorcycle taxi to Cholon, Saigon's Chinatown, to contact my handler, Ms. Kim, and make arrangements to get me back into Cambodia. I needed to get back to Colonel Pham's compound before dark with my reports and photos of the Tết Offensive attacks.

Again, I didn't know if the lady in charge would be there or in a US POW camp—or dead. Everything in my future was unknown at this point. I had to make decisions along the way.

I walked to Ms. Kim's restaurant to find it burned out and destroyed. I found another motorcycle man willing to take me to Cambodia for a price.

*Mr. Long, a Vietnamese man who gave
me food and took me on his motorcycle to Saigon.*

CHAPTER 39
Back to Chiphu, Cambodia

Once in Cambodia, I would be safer. The conflict hadn't melted into this country yet. God, I was hoping to get back to Colonel Pham's compound and have some food and water. A shower would be welcomed. It had been a long and dangerous day.

After a while, we got into the area of Colonel Pham's operation and I asked the motorcycle driver to let me off just around the corner and down the alleyway. I didn't want him to take me to Col. Pham's compound. Once I paid him, I slowly walked around the street, checking things out. So far, the area seemed safe enough for me to enter the compound from a small pathway at the back. They let me in and I was welcomed by Colonel Pham's lieutenant. I asked him his name.

He replied in Vietnamese. "Lieutenant Bien is my name and I have been waiting for your arrival for days. Colonel Pham is at Colonel Gorky's place up near the Laos border. They want to see you right away. I will tell them you are here. I am sure they will decide for you to travel tomorrow morning after breakfast."

"Do you speak French?" I asked in French.

"No, only Vietnamese."

"I speak Vietnamese poorly. My name is Jean Claude."

"I know who you are," Lieutenant Bien said. "People here have been patiently waiting for you, hoping you made it through the Tết Offensive and were not in a hospital or dead somewhere. Colonel Gorky has officially been promoted to brigadier general. He wanted us to tell you right away about his promotion. He is waiting and knows you may have reports about the Tết Offensive in the locations you discussed before you left. I don't have to ask you about your trip. It was very dangerous and risky for you."

"Lieutenant Bien, you must speak slower so I can understand you better," I requested. "I had a few encounters to attend to, and finding my way around was difficult. Getting safe transportation was almost impossible. Places I had to hole up for the night were being bombed. The chaos and suffering of war brought to small farms near villages and their people is tragic."

"Jean Claude, I will call Colonel Pham and tell them you have arrived safely."

"I would like to get something to eat and take a quick shower. I will see them in the morning."

"Let's go out to eat," Lieutenant Bien suggested. "I hear the phone ringing in the office; I must answer it."

"Go ahead. I will wait for you."

Lieutenant Bien returned moments later. "Brigadier General Gorky wants to talk with you."

"I am anxious to speak with him."

I went to the phone and brought it to my ear, switching to French. "Brigadier General Gorky, how are you? I am eager to see you again. Congratulations on your promotion. I want to hear all about this once I am with you."

"Jean Claude," Brigadier General Gorky's voice came through the speaker, "it is wonderful to hear your voice! I am relieved to know you are all right and don't have any injuries. All of us are waiting for your arrival and Angelina is here as well."

"I have been to hell and back. I miss all the conversations around your table and out at the veranda. I am anxious to be with everyone, especially Angelina."

I talked with Brigadier General Gorky and Colonel Pham for a long time. Brigadier General Gorky was sending a helicopter to pick me up at the military location at Phnom Penh's capital airport. I had to call them back in the morning to give them the time I would arrive at the special location at the airport.

Lieutenant Bien planned with an eligible taxi to take me at seven o'clock in the morning. I would comfortably be on the airport helipad by eight. I was looking forward to enjoying good food and having a needed shower. It was the first time in days I had food and showered.

After having breakfast, Lieutenant Bien called Brigadier General Gorky and I spoke with him about several different topics and my arrival time at the helipad. Everything was all in place.

CHAPTER 40

BACK TO PAK NHAI, CAMBODIA

I got to the airport and located the place for my pickup. In just a few minutes, the chopper came and I was on board heading to Brigadier General Gorky's compound. When we arrived, all the staff members, Bopha, Angelina, and Brigadier General Gorky waved at me. All I needed was a band and a red carpet.

It felt like a grand entry with all my friends. Everyone was talking to me at once. All of us were happy to see me intact. We went to the veranda to have a little homecoming celebration. This lasted for hours, and much storytelling was going on with the delicious assortment of snacks and fruity drinks. This went well into the evening. Bopha and Angelina had put together a delightful dinner while all of us were talking about war stories.

"Jean Claude," Brigadier General Gorky said during dinner, "we must get together tomorrow morning after breakfast and go over all the information you have gathered and explain to my staff about the Tết Offensive. The French Embassy in Hanoi has asked that you return there soon. The newspaper in France has many articles for you in Hanoi. They want you to explain and deliver them to different departments of the North Vietnamese government. After I have finalized our day tomorrow, I will plan for you to go to Hanoi."

"I am looking forward to reviewing my trips into Nha Trang with you," I replied. "There were battles going on all around for days. The trip back to Cambodia was very dangerous."

"Jean Claude, my father has told me he can get us a helicopter back to the palace in two days and then to Hanoi," Angelina said.

"Angelina, I would love to do this with you," I replied. "We need to spend time together. It has been a little over one month since we saw each other. I am looking forward to a honeymoon with you."

"I will call my mother and tell her we will arrive soon."

"I can't wait to see your parents and exchange ideas with them. Let's excuse ourselves so I can tell you how much I missed you."

"I thought you would never ask. Of course, we can leave for a short time."

We rose from the table. "Let's go to your villa," I said.

"I don't know if I can wait that long," Angelina exclaimed. "I am anxious to hold you and feel your body close to my mind."

"I'll race you."

We rushed off to Angelina's villa, which was close by. We had her security to deal with, but Angelina knew how to remove them from our general area. It turned out that we were gone for more than just a few minutes. As a matter of fact, Bopha had to come and get us to return for dinner.

"What are you both doing that took so long?" Bopha called.

"I had to show Jean Claude how much I missed him, and in return, Jean Claude showed his passion that he has been waiting to give me," Angelina said. "You know Jean Claude—it took a long time for him to share everything with me."

"Okay, you two lovebirds. Go, they are waiting for you in the dining room."

We got dressed and the three of us rushed off to the dining room to see the other guests clothed very elegantly. I was in clean fatigues and Angelina was dressed casually. But it didn't matter, and cheering ensued. At first, I didn't understand why all the guests were cheering and raising their glasses into the air until Angelina pointed out to me that this was an all-day party for me.

I began to blend into the dining party spirit. All of us had a grand time together, cheering, eating, singing songs, and dancing into the morning hours.

Angelina and I wanted to go to bed early and express our love to each other. We only had two or three days before I left for Hanoi. We decided to let the others continue to enjoy themselves. I had a chance to speak with our host and explain we needed time together. The host excused us and we scurried off to Angelina's villa again, but for the night. Before we left, I gave my sincere appreciation for the homecoming and all the attention that had been rained down upon me. I thanked the host with sincerity.

At breakfast the next morning, most of us sitting around the dining room table looked like we had been up all night, because we had. There was very little talking, just drinking a lot of water and eating food. After finishing our meal, all of Brigadier General Gorky's inner-circle staff, as well as Bopha, Angelina, and I, walked out on the veranda to view the river and absorb last night's events.

Chapter 41
Back to the Palace, Vientiane, Laos

Angelina and I got ready to take the helicopter to the palace in Vientiane. We gave our sincere thanks to Brigadier General Gorky, his staff, all the servants, medical clinic aids, and Bopha.

"Jean Claude, you are welcome anytime," Brigadier General Gorky said. "And I appreciate all the risky missions you have confronted. I did have a speech to read you, but here we are, face-to-face. I can't remember what I wrote down, but you are a very special crusader. You have faced hand-to-hand combat with courageous victory, showed us all what special talents you have inside, your will to live, how you maneuver through danger, and how you change appearances. With all the killing going on in these three countries, you have a shining face of friendship shared with us here. We will miss you, Jean Claude. I salute you."

"It is hard to follow such an exchange of feelings as you have given me," I said. "I want to express my love to each one in this room. All of you have given me special love. I will always carry our experiences close to my heart. One day, I will return to continue our friendship and foster our love. It will grow over time and the forces inside me will guide me back here to rekindle our feelings. Brigadier General Gorky, I want to congratulate you on your promotion to general. It must be that command in Russia was running low on generals and needed to promote *someone* to general, and you were chosen—just joking. In all honesty, you have given me trust and let me be part of an overwhelming part of history many people will never believe nor understand. You have given me a safe haven to become a popular war correspondent. I owe you. I will be back or meet you at another place and time on this earth. In closing, I know you will become a national hero in Russia and with the North Vietnamese government. Without further ado, Angelina and I will fly to Vientiane. Please excuse us, it has been an out-of-this-world experience for me."

Angelina and I finished getting ready, and her security staff went to the helicopter pad. It would be a short flight so we could relax for the rest of the day. We took off and the Gorky staff was waving from below. I would miss their friendship.

When we got close to the helipad at the palace, Angelina's parents and their staff were waiting for us. They greeted us with open arms and smiling faces. It was like a homecoming.

But what would I do about Angelina and her parents? They had adopted me. I needed to move on with my photojournalism profession, go back to France, and move on to my home where my parents and Sofie hadn't heard from me in months. What would my parents, Sofie, and my siblings think of me? I would explain that I wasn't able to write or call them. There wasn't any way I could reach them without revealing my identity. Over time, they would hopefully understand what my MOS detailed and the mission in Vietnam. Maybe I would write my story so they would have a record of my adventure by their bedside to refer to from time to time. If I have a family one day, they, too, could learn about my service to our country.

I was suddenly brought back to the present by Mrs. Vongkhamchanh. "Angelina, Jean Claude, please follow me to the kitchen for a small snack."

"Mother," Angelina said, I missed you while I was gone. Why don't we bring lunch to the table by the pool? Jean Claude and I would like a short swim."

"Ladies, I must say, I have seen carnage throughout Laos, Cambodia, and Vietnam, displaced civilians torn apart by the war. I have been concerned for the safety of Brigadier General Gorky and Prince Vongkhamchanh, Angelina, and all our friends for months. I have seen terrible destruction on my journey to your country. In short, I wish for an end to the war."

Mrs. Vongkhamchanh nodded. "Jean Claude, the prince agrees with you as do I. At dinner, we talked about you and what danger you might have encountered. I am very pleased to see you healthy and with us. God has blessed you!"

"At this time, I express to you my warmest appreciation to your whole family," I said. "You have let me into your family with special permission to court your lovely daughter. It was a long journey before I could make it back to her. Sometimes, it was difficult to maneuver around dangerous encounters. Places were dark and mysterious with deformed people staring at you. I would wonder many times what I was doing in this environment. My heart wanted to be with your family here in Vientiane. Mrs. Vongkhamchanh, could you excuse me just for a little while? I have some other civilian clothes in Angelina's closet. I would be more comfortable around your home in that than in army fatigues."

"Jean Claude, I will call you and Angelina for dinner," Mrs. Vongkhamchanh replied. "We are having a small party tonight with other government officials here in the palace banquet hall, but you and Angelina don't have to attend. Enjoy yourselves in the other dining area off the kitchen. Have fun, enjoy. I am so happy to have you here, Jean Claude."

"I appreciate the confidence and trust you have in me. Not once did you or your family speak in front of me in Laotian. Also, I will take the best care of your daughter. She is a very special lady. She understands the affection I give her. I hear Angelina calling me. Please excuse me, Mrs. Vongkhamchanh."

"Go to her, Jean Claude."

I left Mrs. Vongkhamchanh and went up to Angelina's bedroom. I was surprised to see her lying on top of her bed without any clothes. I closed the door and locked it, checking the other doors. I jumped on top of the bed and embraced her with passionate touches, holding her tightly to me, while trying to get my clothes off. Angelina helped me and they came off at record speed. We locked ourselves together with loving affection that lasted for a long time. Before we could come up for air, Mrs. Vongkhamchanh called us for dinner. Both of us commented on how fast time flies.

"Let's go and eat," Angelina said. "Then we can go for a short walk and rush back to my bedroom. I have been studying the physiology of the male body. I would enjoy experimenting on you tonight. I am going to drive you crazy like you have driven me crazy with the lovemaking you have exposed me to."

"Why eat?" I laughed. "Let's get on with the experiments."

"My mother has dinner for us. We must go, for the servants have prepared the meal. I want us to enjoy the company of my mother and show her we care for our friendship. If we lived alone, we could stay in bed all the time."

"Okay, I can wait, but my feet will touch yours under the table. Just a little foreplay."

"Jean Claude, you are too fresh to be hanging around the palace!" Angelina joked. "I remember dancing with you at the banquet in Hanoi. Your hands were all over my backside. You touched my bottom several times during our dance together. Jean Claude, I enjoyed your touching me. I lived with those touches for several months before I saw you again. You were natural, exciting, and exploring my body like a real man interested in having more of me. I loved it. Other men I danced with at such parties were not exciting at all. My mother was watching you, and she told me that evening after the party to watch out for that Frenchman, for he acted as my father did to my mother on their first night dancing together. My father couldn't stop rubbing her back. Now look at them: he is still touching her like they just met. I think it is wonderful to have parents who display love for each other in front of their children."

"Angelina, I feel like exploring. Your body is perfect. To see you without clothing on top of this bed is exciting and arouses my body."

"Please touch me and turn this body into a romantic mood," Angelina begged. "My body has been waiting for these moments. Tonight, we will stay together as one. I have dreamed of you with me for many months. These dreams I had about us making love seemed real. I would reach out to you to see if I could touch you, to feel your body and bring you close to me again and again. I love that feeling, Jean Claude."

"I have had some experiences dreaming about you," I replied. "I had to be careful because my situation was different. I had to be vigilant and ready to defend myself. I couldn't relax, but I did dream of us often. I was surrounded by people who could potentially hurt or even kill me. One day, I even dreamed about taking you on my journeys, to share with you my history of these missions. It could have been dangerous for me to let my love for you get in the way of my safety. I had to shake my head to come back to reality."

"Let's put that in the past," Angelina said. "Here we are together again. Jean Claude, I want to take a shower with you."

"Only if I can join you and hang on to the soap."

"You are fresh. Come on, let's get wet together."

We showered together with special massaging touches all over our bodies. After a while, we did manage to get into bed again and cuddled for the entire night. Neither of us wanted to face the next morning when news for me to go to the French Embassy in Hanoi would likely come.

But time moved forward, and the sun came up through Angelina's windows. We had one of the best nights of our relationship, but I had to leave her—an exit I didn't want. We had developed strong feelings toward each other. I looked across her nude body, laying on top of the bed so innocently. The sun shone, hitting her body ever so lightly across her back and legs. If I touched her, we would miss the morning meal. We might miss the whole day. But I would always remember her with the sun coming through the windows in her bedroom.

I went to the bathroom for a shower, and Angelina joined me. We ended up in bed for a while, then went downstairs for breakfast. Angelina's parents and family members waited for us. Her mother had a smile on her face like she knew what had been going on upstairs in Angelina's bedroom. I was embarrassed, to say the least.

It was a delightful meal and all of us had our share of laughter. Angelina's father told everyone that my ride to Hanoi would be ready at ten a.m. Once he made this announcement, sadness came across our faces. Angelina started to tear up; her mother began to cry. I held Angelina in my arms and whispered the loving memories we have shared. I told her I would come back or she could visit me in France, or both. I gave her hope, and I wanted her for myself.

After the sadness dwindled around the table, Angelina and I removed ourselves from the table and proceeded to get ready for my departure. It was hard, not only for us but for her family as well. They had to watch as Angelina waited for me to return or call her to come to France.

I didn't know what was in store for me. I had responsibilities for a newspaper in France. If I brought her to France, her security staff would come with her. What was I going to do with them? I would see what was to come with my life when I got to France and had a meeting with Colonel Winter. Until then, I enjoyed myself and gave Angelina my love. I would *wonder* about the life ahead of me.

CHAPTER 42
HEADING TO FRANCE

It was time to leave this dreamland and get back into the field of journalism. The look on Angelina's face broke my heart. I could tell by her expression that she was thinking I would never come back for her. Mrs. Vongkhamchanh gave me all the information to stay in touch with the family, especially Angelina. I protected this information and took photos just in case I lost the papers. I had a five-year visa to visit Laos. I could come and go at will. I didn't think any of my associates in the press corps had access to a private government-owned helicopter. Lucky me!

I got to Hanoi International Airport and went through security. We had a meeting over dinner in the embassy dining area. I had to report for debriefing in the morning at eight a.m. These meetings would last a few days, I was told that evening. Once I was finished with this process, I was to go to France and report to Colonel Winter. Colonel Winter would meet me at the Geneva Airport like before: top level of the parking lot with the vehicle he would drive. This process in France with Colonel Winter would also take a few days. Mostly I had to wait for a US passport, reinstatement as a US citizen and into the US military service. I was told that if I returned to Vietnam or went on a special assignment, I would keep all the French government documents.

I finished all the debriefing formalities within two long days. I wanted to get on my way back to France. I turned in most of the equipment that I was issued at the embassy, and the rest I took back to Colonel Winter in France. I purchased new civilian clothing in Hanoi with the help of the man who had helped me get the right clothing for the banquet. The banquet seemed so long ago. I looked in the mirror and saw a seasoned man who had grown up since I was in this same room fourteen months ago. It felt like a lifetime ago. I now had a few scars, bullet holes, and knowledge about defending myself.

The next morning, I went to the Hanoi International Airport and got on the flight heading to Geneva. I woke up about three hours before landing at the Geneva International Airport. It was a smooth flight and I felt rested. I walked to the top level of the airport parking lot, and there was Colonel Winter, waiting for me in his vehicle. He had a big smile on his face. He got out of his vehicle and gave me a big hug.

"What a spectacular adventure you experienced!" Colonel Winter greeted me in French. "One of the most decorated correspondents that has gone through our training program to date. Get in and let's go to a small welcoming party for you at my office."

"What a surprise," I replied. "I truly appreciate all the support you have given while I was in the field. Colonel Winter, you and your team have given me the best coverage, and I understand the need for secrecy to keep me alive. If anyone along my travels ever found out I was a spy and using journalism as my cover, I wouldn't be here today, rejoicing my return with you. I thank you from the bottom of my heart. I want to also express that my parents and other family members, despite not knowing where I have been these past months, thank you very much for keeping me safe."

"Let's start with our homecoming festivities," Colonel Winter said.

When we arrived at his office, it was full of balloons, ribbons, and staff members I hadn't met yet. As I walked around the room, talking with Colonel Winter's staff, I could see how professional they were. I was convinced his team was well-trained in this specialized field. I remembered the field instructors who beat me up in training lessons, the close combat instructors, the firing range instructors, and the psychological group professors.

The party lasted most of the day, then Colonel Winter came to me and asked if I wanted to go and have dinner at a local restaurant.

"I would enjoy going there with you and maybe bring that lady standing over there near the table. Do you see her?" I asked.

"Jean Claude, you haven't lost the taste of finding lady companionship." Colonel Winter smiled. "Don't you remember Ms. Monet? Our close-combat instructor?"

"Oh really? How close can I get?" I joked.

"I don't know but be careful; she might put you down on your back."

"I will take that chance. How long will I be here with this debriefing?"

"We have already started with some of it," Colonel Winter replied, "and I expect one week. We must wait for new and different travel documents as well as plans on where we will assign you for later duty. I see you have shared with Colonel Black in Nha Trang your two options of interest. Why didn't you include a maid and Asian female cook with your duty at Fort Ord?"

"I wanted to wait and see what you would think about adding those two to the list. You know I will be entertaining foreign officers. If I am signed to the Combat Development Experimentation Command at Fort Ord, my house will be housing these military officers."

"I think you won't have any problems finding help in Monterey and Carmel, California," Colonel Winter said.

"Colonel Winter, I can't wait to get back home and hug my family members."

"Let's wind things up here and move on to the restaurant by the lake," Colonel Winter suggested. "Oh, you better ask the lady to see if she can join us."

"Can I pull rank on her?"

"Go ahead and see if she cares about your rank. By the way, what is your rank?"

"I was going to ask you tomorrow at one of the debriefing sessions." I laughed. "I'm hoping for it to be close to your grade."

"I am not sure myself. I will find out and tell you. I remember in your conversations with Colonel Black you wanted to have a government civilian GS rating."

I nodded. "Yes, somewhere at the level of GS-14 to GS-16."

"You must be dreaming, thinking you are back in Laos or Cambodia living at the Presidential Palace." Colonel Winter smiled. "This is reality here. You will probably be disappointed about your rank."

The close-combat instructor, who introduced herself as Ms. Monet, joined us. The restaurant still looked the same, only the plants were larger. The view across Lake Geneva, toward Lausanne, Switzerland, shone its shadow in the water. Little sailboats danced in the water as they found their way back to their moorings. My feelings came back to me as I stared at the view. I was very fortunate, but I still wondered what was going to come of me.

Finally, I completed all the debriefing formalities and was ready to travel to Boston and embrace my family with big hugs and kisses. I looked forward to my departure in two days.

The next day Ms. Monet took me for a drive in the late afternoon into the nearby mountains. We traveled on the highway to Avoriaz. Along the way, Ms. Monet knew a restaurant where we could have a great meal. She had been here before and knew the employees. I had a juicy steak and real French fries, a cold glass of milk, a fresh salad, followed by homemade vanilla ice cream. I couldn't wait to fill my stomach and taste the juices I had dreamed about while on my assignment in Vietnam.

We returned to Thonon-les-Bains, the city where I would catch the flight to Boston the next morning. I thanked her for the comfortable evening. Ms. Monet told me that Colonel Winter would be taking me to the airport in the morning.

Colonel Winter arrived on time and we left for the airport. At the top-level parking area, we got out of the vehicle, and Colonel Winter surprisingly let me see that he was a down-to-earth person.

"Jean Claude, if you want to come back here and work with us at the training facility, I will put this request on your options for reassignment," Colonel Winter said. "My staff has been observing your professionalism and it would be an honor to have you on board with us.

"This would be a great opportunity for me," I replied. "I will think about this once-in-a-lifetime position. I would enjoy teaching others the art of survival and the complexities of spying. Your staff has shown me great hospitality during my stay. Thank you—thank you for taking the time to show and share with me your experiences while being a spy in Vietnam. Also, Colonel Winter, I am returning the pair of silver chopsticks you let me use while in Vietnam. You are a very important and special person. I have stated this in my reports during the debriefing sessions."

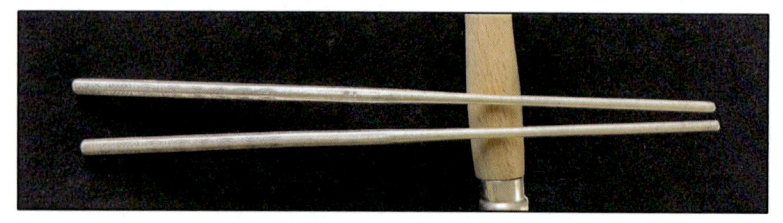

The silver chopsticks Colonel Winter lent me.

I continued. "I have also remarked about your training camp. The things I learned here saved my life many times over. I thank you for my life. I respect you with the utmost regard. I shall never forget my experience here, and especially our relationship. I thank you!"

We hugged each other, and I made my way to check in for my flight.

CHAPTER 43
HEADING FOR BOSTON

Flying to Boston seemed to take forever. I practiced speaking English with anyone who wanted to listen. It was hard remembering the different words I used before going to Vietnam. I decided I would speak slowly when I saw my family and Sofie. Finally, the plane landed and taxied up to the gate. After disembarking, I made it to the waiting area at the gate to happily greet my family. When we finished hugging each other, the floor had enough tear water to float a small boat.

My oldest brother, Paul, his wife, Mary, and my mother were there, but no Sofie Solberg. I was truly upset that Sofie wasn't with the group. I might have been expecting too much since my communication with her while in Vietnam was limited. But I still expected Sofie to be there with open arms. I didn't ask where she was, but I was disappointed. I tried to conceal my sadness and continued to greet my family with happiness.

After the four-hour drive to Vermont, my father, another brother, and his wife were waiting for our arrival in the yard. We had a massive dinner from off the farm where I grew up as a boy. I had a warm and rejoiceful gathering that afternoon and into the evening.

Everyone commented that I needed to rest and relax around the farmhouse before going to bed. Honestly, I wasn't tired. I wanted to find out where Sofie might be and why she wasn't with my family celebrating my homecoming. I tried to sleep but tossed and turned all night, going over all the warm feelings we had before I went to Vietnam. I wanted to rationalize my thinking, but I came up short with my reasoning. I wanted to explain to her face-to-face that I couldn't call her. I had to do things to stay alive so I could go home. I knew she had probably heard that military personnel had R&R leave to meet their loved ones. I decided I would go to Woodstock in the morning to search for her.

I stayed up all night. My parents thought I was deranged, had combat fatigue, and might have problems from the war.

"I want to explain to you that I'm feeling all right," I said to them over breakfast, "and I don't have any emotional or mental scars. I just got back from Vietnam. I need space to see that I am safe and don't have to think about protecting myself. I missed everything you see every day—having a refrigerator in front of me with food and drinks, a bathroom with a shower, a bed with clean sheets, and love from you all.

"Dad, you showed me how to hunt animals and explained to me that hunting for another human being was the real test of hunting skills. I lived with that statement from you the whole time in Vietnam and shared it with fellow soldiers. You have saved my life. I couldn't forget my little beagle dog Chipper, my friend and hunting partner. I remembered outings with Chipper while in the jungles of Vietnam. These memories would give me smiles, while events around me were scenes of hell. But I am home now, eager to get back into the swing of things. I want to revisit friends and see what they are doing and see what I have missed. I am going to Woodstock to look for Sofie. Did Sofie come here to visit you while I was gone?"

"Yes, she did," my mother replied. "I think she came several times in the first six months you were gone. She went to your bedroom and listened to the records. Sofie would have dinner with us on occasion."

"I could hear Sofie softly crying from your bedroom," my father added. "She missed your love and friendship. She asked if we had any news from you every time she could."

"For the last eight months," my mother continued, "we haven't seen or heard from her. We went to Woodstock to check on her but the Smiths weren't helpful and seemed distant. Mrs. Smith was understanding and asked about you."

"If I can use your vehicle, I would like to go to Woodstock and look around, visit some people, and drop in on Mr. and Mrs. Smith," I said. "They will know where Sofie is because the Smiths were responsible for Sofie while she was staying with them. No question they know where she is."

It was almost noon before I left for Woodstock. While I was going over the mountain, I thought about what would happen if I didn't see Sofie or if the Smiths were reluctant to tell me where she had gone. But no matter what, I would have these answers today.

CHAPTER 44
FINDING SOFIE SOLBERG

The first place I went to was the Woodstock Country Club. Sofie enjoyed this place and we met here. I arrived at the parking lot, full of vehicles. There must be a party going on, and Sofie might be here. That would be a surprise for both of us. I made my way into the main banquet hall. People were milling around that I knew. I greeted them and some asked where I was.

"I was on vacation with my rich uncle," I joked, the rich uncle being Uncle Sam.

I made my way over to the bar where my old friend Fred Clark was working. Fred worked as a bartender in the summers and as an accountant at the ski area during the winter months. He was pleased to see me again and said he missed me at the ski area and that many skiers asked about what I was doing. As Fred and I exchanged stories, his brother, Robert Clark, president of the Woodstock National Bank, came over to get a soft drink with ice.

"Are you John?" Robert asked.

"Yes, I am," I replied. "Don't tell me my checking account is overdrawn. I just returned from Vietnam four days ago."

"Oh, no." Robert paused. "John, I have some information to share with you. Can we go outside on the patio for privacy?"

I nodded. "I will follow you."

After we found a corner that was safe to talk, Robert asked, "You know Mr. Richard Smith who has the oil business here in Woodstock?"

"Yes, I know the family but not well," I answered.

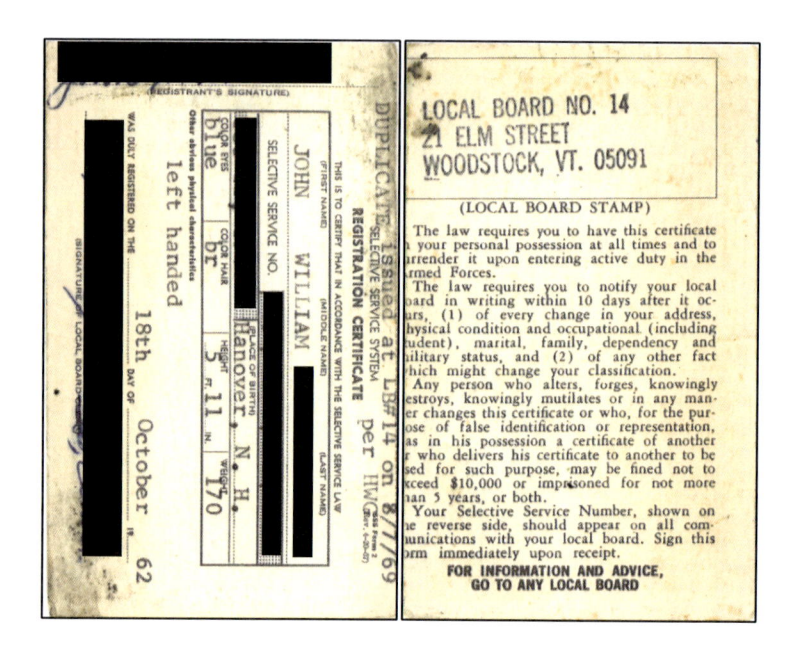

Robert's face was grim and serious. "I was the chairman of the selective service board here in Windsor County for years. Mr. Smith was also on the board and made recommendations for drafting young men into military service. Because you were twenty-two years old at that time, you were red meat for being drafted. Young men much younger than you were being drafted throughout the US. However, here comes the bomb, John: you were having a serious relationship with Sofie Solberg at that time. Mr. Smith was putting your name on the list to be drafted at each meeting. He was adamant about getting you out of Woodstock, into military service, and away from Sofie. Mr. Smith didn't think you should be dating her.

You didn't have the background to be Sofie's lover. Maybe I shouldn't tell you this, but Sofie's parents would keep Sofie's bank account in the healthy six figures. My agreement with her parents was to inform them when Sofie's accounts reached a certain amount; they would transfer funds into her account. I don't know firsthand about her parents' wealth, but it must be substantial."

"Robert, do you know where Sofie is?" I asked with great interest.

Robert shook his head. "I don't know, but I do have her parents' information at the bank. I think I can share some of this information with you. She is not staying with the Smiths anymore. I have heard she was very sad for months waiting for letters or telephone calls from you, but nothing came. Her parents closed the bank accounts, and my bank sent the balance back to Norway."

"You have been very helpful and informative," I told Robert. "I will start searching for her in Norway. However, before I leave Woodstock, I think I will go visit the Smiths and tell Mr. Smith about the adventures I had in Vietnam. I will not tell the Smiths about our conversation today. What was said between us will stay between us."

I thanked Robert again for his help, then returned inside to say goodbye to Fred. I made my way back to the parking lot and drove to the Smiths' home. Their vehicles were parked in the yard, so I went to the front door and knocked. Mrs. Mary Smith came to the door and invited me into the living room. I could see Mr. Smith in his office, obviously stunned by my presence. Mrs. Smith was cordial toward me and asked if I needed anything from the kitchen.

"I just came from the country club," I replied, "and I am full of food and fruit drinks. Thank you anyway. I came here to see Sofie. Is she here?"

Mrs. Smith shook her head. "No, she left several months ago. She hadn't heard from you and there wasn't anything interesting in Woodstock for her. She is living with her parents in Norway and taking advanced college courses."

Mr. Smith finally came crawling out of his cave. I could tell by his body language he was disappointed that nothing terrible happened to me.

"I had a great time with my rich uncle in Vietnam," I said to the rat. "You seem surprised to see me today. I came by to take Sofie away from here."

Mr. Smith was outraged. His complexion turned red, then he turned away from me and walked back into his cave.

"I haven't seen him act like this," Mrs. Smith said. "Why is he so upset about it?"

"Maybe in time, he will explain to you. I think I should leave so you can see to him. Before I leave, I want you to know that I appreciate you letting Sofie live here in Woodstock and for giving her a healthy experience in Vermont as well as allowing her and I to become close friends. Maybe I'll see her again soon. If we get married, can we come by and see you?"

"Sofie and you are welcome here," Mrs. Smith said. "And before you leave, I will give you her parent's address and phone numbers in Norway. They will help you; they're wonderful people."

I thanked her for the information. I felt like I was making progress and headed home. My parents would be pleased that I had this information. I would return home, rest up, and head to Norway to get closure for this lost love or rekindle it by putting new life into it.

I smiled and sang most of the way home. Maybe, just maybe, there was hope for this relationship. Wouldn't that be something to write home about?

When I got home, my mother wanted to know what I had found out.

"I have her address in Norway," I informed her. "I will go there in three days to find her. I need to purchase new clothing before I go and get ready to meet her. What if we get back together again? This time I don't have a Vietnam cloud hanging over my head."

CHAPTER 45
HEADING TO NORWAY

With my US passport in hand, I went to Hanover, New Hampshire, to a travel agency I had used before. I got a flight to Oslo and a train ticket to Bergen. I would leave in two days out of Boston International Airport late in the afternoon. Meanwhile, I planned to get new clothes and a gift for Sofie. I thought I would use a piece of jade I had found in Vietnam and attach it to a gold chain necklace. I planned to find a jeweler in Hanover that would do the work today and have it ready for me tomorrow.

I returned home with my new clothing and rushed to my bedroom to locate the jade piece, then back to Hanover. I gave the jeweler a chance to look at it and see if he could do the setting for me while I waited. So far, things were coming together, and I got what I wanted for the jade piece. The gold chain with the jade was very attractive. With Sofie's taste, I had no doubt she would enjoy wearing it.

My brother Paul, who enjoys driving, took me to Boston in plenty of time. I waited and waited to board the plane. Finally, it was time to go. I was getting anxious and wanted to get going. All the passengers got on and the plane started to move toward the main runway. Then, we were in the air.

I tried to get comfortable and nap, but I was too excited and wanted to arrive in Sofie's town to start my search for her. The vibrations of the plane were like riding in a rocking chair, and I was able to fall asleep. The stewardess woke me up a few minutes before the plane landed in Oslo. I was happy to be awake—one step closer to locating Sofie.

I found the train and headed to Bergen. I couldn't believe I was doing this but I had to see her and find out if we had any sparks left from our romantic past.

Once I arrived at the Bergen train station, I asked for a taxi to take me to Sofie's home. The taxi driver was helpful and took me there very quickly.

Mr. and Mrs. Bjorn Solberg had a very extensive home on the ocean coastline. The property was in a bay, with small boats mooring in the harbor. It was almost as if you could be in Camden, Maine. Just a picture-perfect location.

When I approached the front door, a man came to greet me.

"Is Sofie here at home?" I asked.

"No, she isn't," the man said, "but Mrs. Solberg is in her study."

"Could you tell her that John Wilson from Sharon, Vermont, is here to see her daughter Sofie?"

"Do you have any identification with you?" the man asked.

"Yes," I replied. "I also have a picture of Sofie."

"I will take the picture of Sofie."

I gave him the photo and waited for Mrs. Solberg. In a few minutes, Mrs. Solberg and the gentleman, who was a butler, came to meet me.

"You are the one, John Wilson, who put my daughter's life into a tailspin," Mrs. Solberg said.

"I don't quite follow your meaning," I responded. "I came to see your daughter because I have been away for over a year without communicating with her. I wanted the chance to explain to her why I couldn't reach her. I apologize for any misunderstanding between us, but I am asking for an opportunity to explain to anyone who wants to listen."

"I don't know what to tell you," Mrs. Solberg said, "but the Smiths in Woodstock didn't think very much about your relationship with our daughter. They said you pushed our daughter into doing risqué activities—taking her to parties where drugs were used. I could go on and tell you more about what Mr. Smith said."

"Mrs. Solberg," I replied, "what you have told me is what a jealous old man wanted you to hear. I can tell you things about Mr. Smith, but I am a bigger person. If you, along with Mr. Solberg and Sofie, are still interested in knowing the truth, you may speak with Robert Clark at the Woodstock National Bank. You trust him, and I do too. He will enlighten you about Sofie and our love for each other while she was staying in Woodstock. Furthermore, I didn't expose Sofie to any such activities. We played golf, and tennis, skied together, went out to restaurants, and danced at nice places. Robert will repeat most of the events I have told you about. Can I please see Sofie?"

Mrs. Solberg shook her head. "Sofie is taking courses at a nearby college. She has a different life than what she had in Woodstock. I strongly suggest you leave her alone. She is back on her feet from the heartbreak you gave her. Right now, she has a boyfriend and is happy. Go back to Vermont and leave her alone."

"I am devastated by your comments," I replied. "In short, your thinking is shortsighted. I came here to see Sofie, to explain to her and anyone what happened. I was in a constant position where I couldn't reach out to anyone. Even my family didn't hear from me. I was alone for many months, in danger all the time, sometimes fighting for my life. Mr. Smith and you judge me without hearing my side. I am disappointed to hear your position on this breakup between Sofie and me, but let Sofie decide her fate in our relationship. I believe she will always love me. I have touched her soul with true deep love that no one can match. Having said some of my story, I will leave with honor. Please tell Sofie I came to see her. You owe it to her."

"Mr. Wilson, it is time for you to leave us. Good-bye." Then, Mrs. Solberg closed the door.

I left without incident. As I looked back over my shoulder, the house now seemed like a prison. I walked around in a daze, stunned by my conversation with Mrs. Solberg. The statements made by Mr. Smith in Woodstock floated around too. After a while of walking next to the shoreline in Bergen, I came to realize people in high places think differently. With a little power, they can push other people into their way of thinking. Back in Laos, Cambodia, and Vietnam, there were similar philosophies.

My instinct was to stay around the Solbergs' residence to see if I could spot Sofie returning home. As I sat down on a park bench near Sofie's home, overlooking the shoreline, I remembered having a conversation with one of my nieces. I closed my eyes and started to dream.

"Just look at your life, Uncle Johnnie," my beautiful, God-loving niece Kim Black told me. So, we sat down and wrote the following passage together:

> *"AS I LOOK BACK ON MY LIFE, I MUST STOP AND WONDER... WHY HAVE ALL THESE INTERESTING EVENTS TAKEN PLACE? WHY HAVE I MET ALL THESE FASCINATING*

PEOPLE? ULTIMATELY, WHY HAS MY LIFE TAKEN THIS PATH? IS IT LUCK, FATE, OR IS IT PROVIDENCE, THE HAND OF GOD GUIDING ME? PERHAPS I WILL DISCOVER THE ANSWERS TO THESE IMPORTANT QUESTIONS AS I CONTINUE TO WRITE MY LIFE'S STORY IN MY NEXT BOOK. UNTIL THEN, I WONDER..."

TO BE CONTINUED

JEAN CLAUDE MARTIN

On October 30, 1982, my hometown, Sharon, Vermont, was the first in the United States to erect a Vietnam War memorial. It is located on Interstate I-89 Northbound.

Conclusion

The US and South Vietnamese casualties were around thirteen thousand. After the Tết Offensive, the Viet Cong had massive losses and the NVA supplanted the Viet Cong in military missions in South Vietnam. The Viet Cong went back to small units in rural areas, using ambush, sabotage, and terrorism.

After World War II, the communist regime came to Washington DC asking for support from the US government. At that time, President Dwight D. Eisenhower didn't want to contribute to the Ho Chi Minh cause. The US had just finished the war and France was one of our allies. President Eisenhower's administration reflected their concerns about the domino effect of falling into communism that could happen in Vietnam.

However, Indochina countries—Vietnam, Laos, and Cambodia—already had some form of communist government. Laos and Cambodia supported Ho Chi Minh's ideology on communism. Ho Chi Minh had an army, whereas Laos and Cambodia had small forces but had land and seaports to offer.

China and Russia were slow to come on board with Ho Chi Minh, but they had to because the US was getting more and more actively involved with support for the South Vietnamese region. China didn't want the US close to its borders. China decided to give aid to Ho Chi Minh's region in the form of weapons, rockets, trucks, antiaircraft guns, and surface-to-air missiles, as well as military training to high-ranking officers in the North Vietnamese Army.

Russia couldn't let China be the only one to give support. Reluctantly, they came into Ho Chi Minh's fold, aiding with weapons, jeeps, small trucks, and uniforms.

GLOSSARY

PSP plating: Preference steel plating used for runways and bunkers.

Dien Bien Phu: Location of France's last bloodiest battle and the defeat of Viet Minh by the communist regime; the fall of France's colonies of the Indochina region—Vietnam, Laos, Cambodia.

MOS: Military Occupational Specialty

MACV: Military Assistance Command Vietnam

NVA: North Vietnamese Army

ARVN: South Vietnamese Army

Tết: Lunar new year holiday in Vietnam

VC: Viet Cong had its roots in the 1950s; derived from Viet Nam Cong San (Vietnamese Communists); supporters of North Vietnam's government; military arm of the National Liberation Front (NLF) in 1960; lost its military strength and effectiveness and halted military attacks caused by the massive losses during the 1968 Tết Offensive.

Hue: Ancient capital of Vietnam

Mule: Viet Cong who move supplies to different warehouses

Montagnard: French word for people who live in remote mountain villages.

Acknowledgments

Foremost, all of us must thank the Lord for being there. His loyalty through our lives in bad and good times. In him only absolute peace, positive hope, and eternal love.

I want to express my many thanks to Mr. Cliff Bradshaw, the commissioner of Towns County in Georgia, who reviewed my pictures of my adventures in Southeast Asia. Mr. Bradshaw encouraged me to write my story and have it published. I thank you for your continued support, Mr. Bradshaw.

To my friend Dr. Emily Jean Darraj who reviewed my notes and gave me advice on how to weave my story into an interesting book. She is an accomplished author who stepped up and helped.

I want to thank all the editors at BookLogix for taking the time to advise me on the general layout of the book. BookLogix editors combed my manuscript and massaged the chapters into a smooth-flowing story. Many thanks to the book cover designer who illustrated the story to help bring the attention of potential readers. Our many meetings were very helpful in producing this book.

I must thank my niece, Kim, and her husband, Greg Black, for the encouragement they gave me along this journey. Their many friends at Prestonwood Baptist Church in Plano, Texas, enveloped me with love that I found irresistible and charming. The church complex is a large, magnificent facility with thousands of members, they made me feel welcome and loved as if I was the only person in their midst—a special thanks to their friend Parker Eng.

A loud shout goes to Colonel Dima Gorky's friendship and the memorable trust we built between us during this conflict in Southeast Asia. I give you a Roman Soldier's handshake!

I want to thank all U.S. military and non-military personnel who served our country during the Vietnam War for their secretary, support, and effort to save front-line combatants' lives.

I want to thank all the medical personnel who served in the Vietnam War for the brave attention given to all the service men and women who required their skills.

I want to thank all the military and non-combatant people in North and South Vietnam, Laos, and Cambodia for their helpfulness, for making friendships, and for allowing me to perform my missions while their country was in turmoil.

I can't forget to thank all the people behind my missions whom I never met and who aided in my success in completing the objective. I salute you!

I want to thank all Vietnam veterans for the sacrifices that they and their families have made for the freedoms that we all cherish today.

To my friend Mr. Tim McHugh who has supported this idea of writing my story and publishing it. I thank him for his continued interest in the success of this book by telling people about my story.

To Jack H. Wilson who was helpful with any software issues while writing the manuscript.

I want to thank all the readers who choose my book to understand another side of the Vietnam War. How the war strategy was orchestrated in neighboring countries to be on offense while the US forces were on defense. To read about all the anguish that war brings to the non-combatant population in their country.

About the Author

Jean Claude Martin was born in Hanover, New Hampshire, and raised in Sharon, Vermont, a small village with 200 residents. He attended a college in Vermont.

In 1966, Jean Claude enlisted for miliary service. He served during the Vietnam War, traveling to most locations in South Vietnam as a combat photographer. Jean Claude's service gave him exposure to the Russian Airforce and US Airforce airstrikes. With a photography background, he captured film of the airstrikes in a way that hadn't been done before.

In his late twenties, he became a ski area manager and ski school director at a major ski resort, skiing France, Italy, and Switzerland's ski resorts. During the summer months, he worked in a French ski factory.

Jean Claude went back to Vietnam in 1999 and started doing business and exporting goods in Vietnam, giving him the chance to visit locations where he witnessed combat and saw the scars of war washed away. He has been back many times since and has seen modernistic improvements. Today, new buildings and major developments have sprouted up with modern designs in the cities throughout Vietnam.

Some of Jean Claude's hobbies are fishing, deer hunting, scuba diving, and camping, and he enjoys traveling to different countries and learning about their cultures. He travels to places like Vietnam, Cambodia, Laos, Chine, Japan, Mongolia, all over Europe, and Turkey, and has had memorable experiences in these countries and with their citizens. Some of his favorite places to visit are Da Lat, Phan Tuyet, and numerous Montagnard villages. In Laos, the country has many Montagnard villages to visit. Southeast Asia is truly a location that is worthy of visiting.